MW00678723

STAND
AND BE
COUNTED

STAND
AND BE
COUNTED

A Washington Insider
Tells How to Preserve America's Liberties
for You and Your Children

Robert Dugan

MULTNOMAH BOOKS · SISTERS, OREGON

STAND AND BE COUNTED
© 1995 Robert P. Dugan

Published by Multnomah Books
a part of the Questar Publishing Family

Edited by Matt Jacobson
Cover design by Bruce DeRoos
Cover photo by Liason International
Sandra Baker

Printed in the United States of America.

International Standard Book Number: 0-88070-783-6

Unless otherwise indicated, all Scripture references are from the
Holy Bible: New International Version, copyright 1973, 1978, 1984 by
the International Bible Society.
Used by permission of Zondervan Bible Publishers.

All rights reserved.
No part of this publication may be reproduced, stored in a retrieval
system, or transmitted, in any form or by any means, electronic,
mechanical, photocopying, recording, or otherwise, without prior
written permission. For information:
Questar Publishers, Inc.
Post Office Box 1720
Sisters, Oregon 97759

95 96 97 98 99 00 01 02 03 — 15 14 13 12 11 10 9 8 7 6 5 4 3 2 1

CONTENTS

DEDICATION

To my namesake grandson, Robert Perry Dugan, IV
with the prayer that his country
will have determined to remain "One Nation Under God"
long before A.D. 2011
when he will first be eligible to vote.

FOREWORD

Bob Dugan would have made a great congressman. He's smart, energetic, meets people well, and has a voice that resonates with authority. He is also an excellent public speaker with a flair for clearly and persuasively stating his case on complex issues of public policy.

So it was only natural that Bob would run for office, and in 1976 he did so, becoming a candidate for the United States House of Representatives. Had he won the election, it could have been the start of a brilliant political career.

But this book might never have been written.

Thoughtful Christians, especially those of us who are alarmed about the moral depravity of our days, have good reason to be thankful this book was written. Let us hope it will be widely read and acted upon by believers everywhere.

It turned out that the Lord did not plan for Bob to become a Congressman, at least not in 1976. Instead Bob was called to the nation's capital to head the Office of Public Affairs of the National Association of Evangelicals. In that capacity, he has become one of America's leading strategists and spokesmen on moral, legislative, and political issues of concern to Christians.

Most of us, especially followers of Jesus Christ, are concerned. We realize that America, despite its greatness and freedom and prosperity, is deeply troubled. Thoughtful citizens can scarcely ignore the grisly toll that suicide, abortion, divorce, drugs, pornography, homosexuality, secularism, cheating, and cynicism have had on our beloved country.

Our Lord asked, "What will a man be profited if he gains the whole world but forfeits his soul?"

Many of us think the same principle applies to our nation. What is the profit to America if we have endless economic prosperity, computers and a hundred channels of television in every home, new cars, boats, glamorous vacations, and more...if our families are shattered, our children are corrupted; if we forget or throw away the values and traditions that are the soul of America; or worst of all, if we Christians fail to honor Jesus Christ?

Bob Dugan meets such issues head-on with faith, optimism, and a firm intention to reclaim America's heritage of biblical values. He demonstrates how a person can fight for principle in the political world without compromising his testimony.

Firmly rooted in the Bible, the U.S. Constitution, and a wealth of practical experience, this book gives believers a solid grounding on major issues, a framework for strategy, and a battle plan for honoring God in the political process.

In this book, Bob Dugan is not seeking merely to entertain or engage your attention. He wants to change your life. He intends to recruit and motivate you to help turn things around for America.

I pray he will be successful in doing so.

Former Senator Bill Armstrong
Washington, D.C.

WHAT

THE

TIMES

REVEAL

Chapter One

HOW GRAVE IS AMERICA'S MORAL DECLINE?

ost Americans, in their grandest dreams, can't imagine themselves in the same room with the president of the United States. For the comparative few who make it into his presence, that room will most likely be a hotel ballroom seating more than one thousand. Even then, a chance to shake the president's hand will be only a remote possibility, much less an opportunity to say anything meaningful to him.

In God's providence, however, for more than sixteen years meeting with presidents has been no novelty for me. I've been privileged to represent evangelical Christians in the nation's capital, in the process frequently meeting in small groups with Presidents Carter, Reagan, Bush, and Clinton. Still, I surprised myself in the summer of 1990 at my audacity insisting on a meeting with President George Bush. Without repeatedly ringing the doorbell at 1600 Pennsylvania Avenue, I had come close to demanding an invitation into the White House.

There was plenty of reason for such a meeting. In April, now-retired Senator Bill Armstrong of Colorado, keynoting NAE's Washington Insight Briefing, reported that on that very afternoon the president had entertained a group of homosexual activists at a White House bill-signing ceremony. "It gives them a status they have never previously received," he said, "and undermines the pastors and youth workers who are trying to hold the line against immorality." Having already phoned the president himself to protest, he urged us to express ourselves in the strongest terms through letters and calls to the White House comment line. We did.

Then, to our doubled distress, word of a second White House invitation to gay activists leaked out in mid-summer. Incredibly, a group whose sole reason for existence is to justify, advocate, and gain societal and governmental approval for an immoral lifestyle, had been invited back. *The Washington Blade*, a gay newspaper, was quick to crow about having some of its people again included at the White House. They were well aware of the significance of the precedent, even if the president seemed oblivious to it.

Southern Baptist leader Richard Land was my chief co-belligerent in pressing, week after week, for a confrontation with President Bush. In round numbers, the National Association of Evangelicals and the Southern Baptist Convention each represented about fifteen million people, and our support was critical enough to George Bush that White House staff granted our meeting. It would have been a grave political error to ignore the legitimate complaint of such a constituency.

Most of the eighteen evangelical leaders who headed for the White House that October 30 spent two hours at our Washington office in preparation and prayer. They were determined not only to warn the president that his relationship with evangelicals had deteriorated to the point of being "on the ropes," but also to offer positive suggestions on how the relation-ship could be repaired.

As we walked the three blocks to the White House, I remembered the times I heard Nixon administration special counsel, Charles Colson, chuckle about how he had disarmed the anger of group upon group during his White House years. He treated them to a taste of what others have called "the imperial presidency," through a meal in the White House Mess, glimpses of political celebrities, hushed tones, and even drop-in Oval Office conversations with President Nixon himself.

"Invariably," writes Colson, "the lions of the waiting room became the lambs of the Oval Office." Noting that "most forgot their best-rehearsed lines," Colson added, "Ironically, none were more compliant than the religious leaders."[1] After twelve years in Washington, the novelty had worn off. That would not happen to me.

CONFRONTING PRESIDENT BUSH

We were seated in large leather chairs around the polished con-ference table in the softly lit Roosevelt Room, right across the hall from the Oval Office. The dialogue was frank enough that the atmosphere at times became tense. Richard Land opened the conversation by speaking of a "serious erosion in his [the presi-dent's] support among evangelicals." Land candidly listed three "flash points" that were causing disappointment, confusion, and concern: "Invitations to homosexual rights activists to attend bill-signing ceremonies at the White House; the administration's failure to seek restrictions on controversial grants given by the National Endowment for the Arts; the need for stronger and more visible leadership from the president on the abortion issue."

Even before we began there was a shadow that hung over this meeting. Doug Wead, friend to many during the Bush election campaign and, as an evangelical, liaison to our religious community, had been fired on September 1. He had accused several White House staffers of not serving the president well and also wrote to evangelical leaders to explain the summer's developments regarding the gay activists. For that, the axe fell.

In any case, when Richard had finished his forceful paragraphs he yielded the floor to "the gentleman from NAE." "Mr. President," I began, "gay rights activists have an agenda. Their goal is to make this final decade of the twentieth century the Gay Nineties in a sense totally unthinkable a century ago, when gay meant lighthearted and carefree." I pointed out that homosexuals had been granted tacit recognition by his administration at two bill-signing ceremonies, something even gay activists had never anticipated in their wildest dreams, and certainly not in the Bush administration. "If they succeed," I continued, "then God Almighty is either going to have to judge the United States or apologize to Sodom and Gomorrah."

The president's comment was strained. "I was not overly thrilled when that [the invitations to gay activists] happened. A signal was put out that we're condoning that lifestyle, which caused an understandable uproar." At best, it seemed to me a lame response.

That day I sensed I had stood in the tradition of the Old Testament prophets. I had spoken firmly, frankly, and faithfully to America's equivalent of the king of Israel.

Just before we left the White House I handed the president a sealed packet with more than a dozen glossy eight-by-ten-inch photographs from the homoerotic Mapplethorpe art exhibit, disgracefully funded through the National Endowment for the

Arts—by the tax dollars of decent American taxpayers. More of that in Chapter 10.

For now, fast-forward to April 1993. Bill Clinton has been in office as president nearly three months. He is seated in the Oval Office with several White House staffers and eight gay and lesbian activists. Seizing an opportunity to open the conversation, one homosexual boldly spoke: "Well, Mr. President, welcome to the Gay Nineties." It was reported that the president laughed uproariously.

Governmental acceptance of homosexuality is no laughing matter. Rockford Institute founder, John Howard, did not carelessly write, "With the family unit already weakened and scorned by the dominant culture, the President now proposes the dismissal of heterosexual marriage as the national norm and the validation of homosexuality as a fully acceptable and comparable living pattern."[2]

The time has come to ask ourselves a pivotal question: Did America's 1992 elections inaugurate not only Bill Clinton, but also the triumph of cultural radicalism? One internationally known evangelical leader apparently thought so, admitting that he caught himself using the term "post-Christian America" for the first time on November 4, 1992, the day after election day. What a sobering assessment.

In your mind's eye, go back with me to Philadelphia, more than two centuries ago. When the Founding Fathers met in their 1787 Constitutional Convention, they soon determined that the Articles of Confederation under which they had been operating were inadequate for a national government. As they set out to "invent" a new nation, they agreed to do so in utmost secrecy. George Washington one day scolded the delegates when a written resolution was found carelessly dropped on the floor: "I must entreat, gentlemen, to be more careful lest our transactions get into the News Papers and disturb the public repose by premature speculations."

But the columnists and commentators of the eighteenth-century news media must have been abject amateurs compared to those of our time. It seems incredible that when the convention was over, an old lady could accost Benjamin Franklin just outside the doors of Philadelphia's Constitution Hall and ask: "Well, Dr. Franklin, what have we got, a Republic or a Monarchy?" Franklin's reply became a classic: "A Republic, Madam, if you can keep it."[3]

For over two hundred years we have managed to maintain that Republic, through terribly difficult times of testing, including a Civil War, two World Wars, the Great Depression, and a fiercely unpopular war in Vietnam. Now, in the mid-1990s, the United States of America confronts as severe a test as the nation has ever faced, although some Americans, unbelievably, scoff at such an assertion and express pleasure at the direction our culture is moving. That does not surprise me. It is a timeless truth that "there is a way that seems right to a man, but in the end it leads to death" (Proverbs 14:12).

AMERICA'S CULTURE WAR

Our nation's cultural drift has brought us to a crisis serious enough to be called a "culture war." If my basic premise is correct, that Almighty God, the Maker of heaven and earth, is the ultimate umpire among the nations, then losing the war of values could find Americans scouring library shelves for *The Decline and Fall of the Roman Empire*—to discover where we went wrong.

Others have seen the culture war for the soul of America coming. In 1988, America's leading evangelical theologian, Carl

F. H. Henry, wrote *Twilight of a Great Civilization*. He was speaking of ours, not that of the ancient Hittites.

> In a culture dominated by a neo-pagan mind and will, deviation tends to become the norm, and normalcy in turn is perversely declared deviant. That cultural condition is the midnight hour for an evangelical alternative... before the collapse and ruination of the contemporary social scene.[4]

In 1989, Charles Colson wrote *Against the Night: Living in the New Dark Ages*. He sensed then that a "crisis of immense proportions is upon us," and mentions others with similar foreboding.

> Malcolm Muggeridge predicts the end of Christendom. Francis Schaeffer warns of the spiritual collapse of the West. Even secular journals sound the alarm. *Newsweek* declares "the American century...over," and *Time* declares a "moral malaise overhanging American life."

> ...the crisis that threatens us...is in the character of our culture, where the values that restrain inner vices and develop inner virtues are eroding. Unprincipled men and women, disdainful of their moral heritage and skeptical of Truth itself, are destroying our civilization by weakening the very pillars upon which it rests.[5]

In 1990, addressing the annual convention of National Religious Broadcasters, psychologist Dr. James Dobson said, "We are engaged at this time in an enormous civil war of values." He portrayed Judeo-Christian values at loggerheads with a humanistic, avant-garde perspective that recognizes no absolute values, adding: "What most people don't realize is that our children are the prize. Those who control what children see, hear and are taught control the nation."

A *New York Times* feature on Dobson and Focus on the Family reported that his ministry generates an average of ten thousand letters per month, many heart-wrenching. "'Through this department we are watching the unraveling of a social order,' Dr. Dobson said. 'Five years ago people wrote us about thumb-sucking and bed-wetting. Now they're writing about wife beating, child abuse, manic depression, suicide and satanic cults.'"

In 1991, I borrowed Dr. Dobson's graphic civil war terminology to title my new book *Winning the New Civil War: Recapturing America's Values.* One reviewer's sole criticism hinged on the title's first word. Apparently I was naive enough to believe that the culture war could still be won.

Call me naive if you wish. But read this book first. I believe I know who only can prevail in the struggle to reverse the disintegration of America's culture. While the United States of America is now the world's only superpower combining military, economic, and political leadership, its people cannot afford to live at nonchalant ease, oblivious to the danger of the collapse of their culture. It is not unthinkable that God may before long write Ichabod (1 Samuel 4:21) over our society. It happened to his chosen nation of Israel. The truly naive are those who think and act as if it couldn't happen to us.

Evangelical Protestants are not the only people who understand the crisis. Catholic theologian Avery Dulles, a Harvard-trained lawyer and son of one-time Secretary of State John Foster Dulles, said that the culture war "ultimately...could bring the collapse of democracy. It's gone pretty far." Associated Press religion writer George Corness reported his argument:

> "Two visions of the American political experiment are struggling for supremacy," said Dulles. The once-prevailing view that democratic rule depends on people recognizing God-given principles of justice and morals is now pitted against a view that the nation is not bound to any fixed truths or morality.

> "Anything funded by the government has to be stripped of religious conviction," he said. "You can believe in Marx or anything else, but you can't mention God. In effect, we're establishing secularism. That's what makes it difficult to maintain any moral climate in the country as a whole."[6]

One could never accuse Senator Daniel Patrick Moynihan (D-NY) of pandering to the Religious Right, but he comprehends the situation. On April 15, 1993, the liberal New York senator infuriated the political establishment when he addressed the Association for a Better New York, deploring the deterioration of the quality of life and adding, "The amount of deviant behavior in America has increased beyond the levels the community can afford to recognize." What a tragedy when a society "defines deviancy down," accepting what we once regarded as repulsive.

William Bennett, a cabinet member during both the Reagan and Bush administrations, sarcastically wrote that "there once was a time when personal failures, subliminal desires, and perverse taste were accompanied by guilt or embarrassment. Today these are a ticket to appear on the Sally Jessy Raphael show."[7]

A year before, Bennett had released the most comprehensive statistical portrait of behavioral trends made available over the last thirty years, "The Index of Leading Cultural Indicators."[8] By contrast, leading economic indicators during that period were very strong. With a population increasing 41 percent since 1960, the Gross Domestic Product nearly tripled, and total social spending by all levels of government rose more than five times.

Socially, however, the facts were depressing. During that same period violent crime rose by 560 percent, both illegitimate births and divorce rates increased by 400 percent, the percentage of children living in single-parent homes tripled, the teenage suicide rate more than doubled, and college entrance exams saw a drop of almost 80 points in average scores. This inventive report, which includes a dozen other cultural indicators, has blown the whistle on American culture. And when Bennett calls attention to the "enormous human cost" of our social regression and decomposition, our nation needs ears to hear.

Politically, there have been two great tragedies in this century, according to astute conservative leader Paul Weyrich. In one, the State became God. Now, we watch a greater tragedy develop in our nation, as man attempts to become God. Weyrich buttresses his argument by pointing to humanity's seizing, through Congress and the courts, the Creator's right to control life and death. The scientific technologies of abortion and euthanasia make perfectly good sense to secular reasoning.

FIVE DISTINCT DECADES

How have we come to this in the United States? I turn to a China-born, England-educated sociologist for a sketch of the second half of the twentieth century. In his monumental book *The American Hour: A Time of Reckoning and the Once and Future Role of Faith*, Os Guinness labels the fifties as a decade of high confidence, the last period marked by the pillars of social stability, moral legitimacy, and economic prosperity.

The sixties became one of the five major periods of break-down in American history, with all three pillars shattered. The assassinations of John F. Kennedy, Martin Luther King Jr., and Bobby Kennedy, the war in Vietnam, and the counterculture movement, which included a sexual revolution, ushered in a "post-Christian era" not fully fathomed at the time. The cultural revolution was most painfully distinguished by a wide-ranging rejection of authority.

The seventies became the "me decade" but included "the year of the evangelical" and the emergence of a tough kind of political activism that would characterize the New Religious Right. Guinness quotes a neo-liberal who described President Carter's White House Conference on Families as a "festival of rel-ativism under whose guidelines even a fraternity house officially qualified as a family."[9] No wonder the new activism.

The eighties then developed into a gilded era during which Americans lived beyond their means and in which a potent evan-gelical voting bloc surfaced. That confederation was roundly resisted and resented by secularists.

The nineties find our culture in a crisis of authority.

Recounting his deliverance from the bonds of secularism in *After Modernity, What?*, Thomas Oden points out "a modern chauvinism that assumes the intrinsic inferiority of all pre-modern thought and the consequent superiority"[10] of any contemporary idea. This chauvinism is named Modernity. The word has more to do with an attitude than with chronological time. It silently assumes that anything new, ipso facto, is good, and that change automatically deserves to be considered improvement. Its goal is one of liberation from all restrictions and restraints. For Modernity, traditional values are highly suspect and the idea of a revealed, written, authoritative Word of God is, frankly, repugnant and stupid.

Before Bill Clinton had been in the Oval Office very long, most Americans realized that this president was quite unlike any before him. He was the first president educated during the sexual and cultural revolution of the sixties—the Vietnam era. He was the first "baby boomer" to be elected chief executive.

At 30 percent of the population, the baby boom generation (Americans born between 1946 and 1964) is our largest and best-educated generation. The stereotypical boomer tends to be self-indulgent and quite sure that his generation is brighter than any other. The *Wall Street Journal* suggests that boomers as a generation have a special, abiding concern for gay and abortion rights.

BILL CLINTON IN THE OVAL OFFICE

If it is fair to suggest that Bill Clinton is a product of change, it also seems fair to suggest that President Clinton is a producer of change. Southern Baptist or not.

Take the matter of abortion. On January 22, his second day in office and the anniversary of the ignoble *Roe v. Wade* abortion-on-demand decision, he undid most of the pro-life gains of the prior twelve years, by an in-your-face series of executive orders. Likewise with the issue of homosexuality. Although he would later be rebuffed by Congress and the American people, against the advice of our armed forces' leadership, Clinton kept his promise to initiate a policy concerning gays in the military.

At their convention that June, Southern Baptists reported that half of their proposed resolutions targeted President Clinton. One evangelist said, "We are like the father of the Prodigal Son, waiting and praying with the porch light on, ready to run to meet Clinton halfway down the road."[11] The president's starting Inauguration Day at a prayer meeting and concluding it at gay and lesbian parties was more than a little disturbing.

One need not be a theologian to realize that something as fundamental as two of the Ten Commandments are for the first time under attack by the administration of a president of the United States.

The sixth commandment, "You shall not kill," is being violated 1.5 million times each year through abortion. I cannot imagine a more powerful public rebuke than that delivered by that tiny wisp of a woman, Mother Teresa of Calcutta, at the 1994 National Prayer Breakfast. She opened her address by speaking of God's love, manifested in Jesus' death on the cross, and our duty to love the most needy in turn. Then she shifted gears. "But I feel that the greatest destroyer of peace today is abortion, because it is a war against the child, a direct killing of the innocent child, murdered by the mother herself. And if we accept that a mother can kill even her own child, how can we tell other people not to kill one another?"

Much of the audience stood to its feet, applauding for almost a full minute. Many of us felt that we had witnessed a prophetic confrontation comparable to the prophet Nathan's "You are the man," spoken to King David. Some in the audience were angry that Mother Teresa had the effrontery to speak of what they felt to be a controversial subject. A few whispered their worry that embarrassing the Clintons, in full view at the head table, might jeopardize their participation at future prayer breakfasts. It occurred to me at the time that some night, when sleep was elusive, God's spirit might use Mother Teresa's words to convict the president, so that he would change his mind about his abortion policies.

The seventh commandment, "You shall not commit adultery," is also under brazen assault in America today. No student of the Bible should conclude that only heterosexual sin is in view here. The Westminster Larger Catechism gives a comprehensive catalogue of prohibited sexual behaviors. "The sins forbidden in the Seventh Commandment, besides the neglect of the duties required, are adultery, fornication, rape, incest, sodomy, and all unnatural lusts; all unclean imaginations, thoughts, purposes, and affections…"

Further, no biblical chapter could be clearer on the subject of homosexuality than the first chapter of Romans. Verses 18 through 23 speak of perverted minds that "suppress the truth by their wickedness" and of "foolish hearts [being] darkened. Verses 24 though 31 speak of perverted bodies, three times reinforcing that "God gave them over" to "the degrading of their bodies," to "shameful lusts," and "to do what ought not to be done." Finally, verse 32 speaks of perverted wills that, "Although they know God's righteous decree that those who do such things deserve death, not only continue to do these very things but also approve of those who practice them."

Even people with a limited knowledge of the Bible know the fate of Sodom and Gomorrah, recorded first in Genesis and reiterated in 2 Peter 2:7-10 (with a parenthetical Jude 7):

> If he condemned the cities of Sodom and Gomorrah by burning them to ashes, and made them an example of what is going to happen to the ungodly…(In a similar way, Sodom and Gomorrah and the surrounding towns gave themselves up to sexual immorality and perversion.)…the Lord knows now to rescue godly men from trials and to hold the unrighteous for the day of judgment, while continuing their punishment. This is especially true of those who follow the corrupt desire of the sinful nature and despise authority.

A TWENTIETH-CENTURY CRISIS OF AUTHORITY

Note well those last words. Those who "despise authority" are aiding and abetting our contemporary crisis of authority—our culture war. They are dead set against the Judeo-Christian consensus that our Founding Fathers determined to make foundational in our kind of society.

Tragically, in the interests of diversity, the current administration has placed cultural radicals in positions of great public influence. That has led, for example, to affirmative action in the hiring of homosexuals in various agencies and in the White

House; to Gay Pride days being celebrated in certain departments; and to administration GLOBE chapters, gay, lesbian, or bisexual employees organizations. In the summer of 1994 it was announced in the Department of Agriculture that departmental offices would be reimbursed, at taxpayers' expense, for transportation to attend events surrounding Gay and Lesbian Pride Month.

An unabashed secularist agenda will be promoted by the Clinton administration, unless the president undergoes a drastic change of heart. His appointees will see to that. Consider Thomas Payzant, assistant secretary of education for elementary and secondary education. In his days as superintendent of San Diego's public school system, he satisfied homosexual activists by forcing the Boy Scouts out of the schools, saying, "We can't tolerate an organization like that influencing young people."[12]

Another Clinton appointee is Roberta Achtenberg, former San Francisco Bay Area county supervisor and lesbian activist, now assistant secretary for fair housing and equal opportunity in HUD, the Department of Housing and Urban Development. A few years ago she represented San Francisco bathhouse patrons in their battle against efforts to close them down after the AIDS crisis became a serious public health problem, arguing that the bathhouses were a "sex positive environment." At her Senate confirmation hearing, she had the temerity to introduce her lesbian lover to the committee. The senators applauded, later confirming her by 58 to 31.

The now notorious former surgeon general, Joycelyn Elders, served in Bill Clinton's Arkansas cabinet as director of health while he was governor. The president's judgment is still under scrutiny for appointing her as surgeon general of the United States. In repeated outrageous remarks that could fill a chapter in this book, Elders used her federal platform to insult religious citizens and make light of their convictions. America needs to "get over its love affair with the fetus," she snidely remarked. Having educated our teens in what to do in the front seat of a car through driver education, Elders wanted to show them what to do in the back seat, with condoms. She created a climate of permissiveness and experimentation, encouraging sexual activity of all kinds, at ages much too young to be taking driver's ed.

Elders knows few boundaries in celebrating permissiveness. Following her appointment, she spoke several times favorably about the possible legalization of drugs. Having her way would have eased the predicament of her twenty-eight-year-old son, Kevin, who insisted his parents knew of his drug habit. The prosecutor sought a ten-year prison sentence after Kevin sold cocaine to an undercover police officer in Little Rock while Elders insisted that what he did was no crime.

The surgeon general wanted the Boy Scouts to drop their ban on homosexual leaders, and in an interview with the gay magazine the *Advocate*, she endorsed homosexual adoptions and called homosexual sex "normal and healthy." It is nothing short of scandalous that America's most influential medical doctor could call gay sexual activity "healthy," not to mention "normal." Was she ignorant of the spread of AIDS, which even gays acknowledge to be spread primarily through homosexuality in the United States?[13] How long can our nation tolerate such madness?

Decent, reasonable Americans wondered if there was anything outrageous enough Elders could say that the White House would demand her resignation. It finally happened. On December 9, two years into his presidency, Bill Clinton fired her without allowing her the face-saving gesture of writing a letter of resignation. She should never have been appointed in the first place.

Polls are showing that three of every four Americans believe their nation is in moral and spiritual decline. Two of every three think their country is seriously off track.

HOW WILL THE CULTURE WAR END?

George Weigel, president of Washington's Ethics and Public Policy Center, states, "All that is necessary for a good democracy is a virtuous people."[14]

Fortunately, many upright Americans have begun to realize that the future depends on them. A significant percentage of those virtuous people are evangelical Christians, submissive to the authority of their Creator, who endowed them with certain inalienable rights. They understand that "when the righteous thrive, the people rejoice; when the wicked rule, the people groan" (Proverbs 29:2). It is self-evident to them that moral leaders will not be placed in office by immoral people, and most assuredly not by cultural radicals who absolutely reject Judeo-Christian values. This explains why evangelicals are becoming increasingly active in the political arena.

Statistics from 1994 proved that evangelicals had caught on to the relationship between their duties as citizens and the cultural crisis. In those off-year elections, evangelicals more than doubled their participation of four years before, becoming perhaps the most important political factor in the outcome. According to the Bliss Institute on Applied Politics at the University of Akron, evangelicals comprised 33 percent of the total electorate—a huge leap upward from their modest 15 percent in 1990.

The results showed it. Angry voters, with almost surgical precision, focused their resentment on the president, his party,

and their liberal political philosophy. Veteran Democratic strate-
gist Mark Shields candidly affirmed that "Clinton was the issue."
Political guru Kevin Phillips wrote that "the Republican seizure
of Congress for the first time in forty years is also the century's
biggest repudiation of the newly elected president in his first
midterm elections." A full evaluation of the significance of 1994
follows in Chapters 8 and 10.

It is not impossible that Americans may someday point to
November 8, 1994, as pivotal—the day a tidal wave of change
began to roll over our nation, wiping out the cultural radicalism
that threatened to destroy us. On the other hand, 1994 could be
just a two-year eddy in the surf, leading back to perilous years of
political undertow. No one can predict which it will be.

Everything hinges on virtuous people bringing others into
the process with them who will elect Congresses and presidents
(who in turn appoint Supreme Court justices) who share their
vision for a restored America. How to do it? That's what the suc-
ceeding nine chapters are all about.

WE, GOD'S PEOPLE

Evangelicals must surely be praying for God's mercy on the
United States of America. They do so with a marvelous promise:
"If my people, who are called by my name, will humble themselves and pray and seek my face and turn from their wicked
ways, then will I hear from heaven and will forgive their sin and
heal their land" (2 Chronicles 7:14).

Even though this promise was made by God directly to the
Children of Israel at a specific moment in history, it has general
application to us today. Make no mistake. There are four conditions that must be met by God's people (not by all Americans).
Spiritual and political renewal will not come unless all four criteria

are met. The first three conditions are matters of personal piety: *if* my people will humble themselves, *if* my people will pray, and *if* my people will seek my face. The fourth criterion is often overlooked: *if* my people will turn from their wicked ways.

Somehow this final condition seems unsuited to God's people. After all, turning from wicked ways requires repentance, a new direction. But there can be a direct application for many of us. Let's face it. Evangelicals' most common political sin is not one we commit but one we omit. More often than not we have been aloof from politics, uncaring about the culture war, selfishly tending to our own interests. Even if we have been praying, we've probably omitted participating.

The time for ignorance and apathy is over. Our culture will degenerate into godless oblivion if Christians remain on the political sidelines. We must choose active involvement. It is then conceivable that God will be willing to hear from heaven and heal our land.

WHAT DO WE "KNOW" THAT JUST ISN'T SO?

Although evangelicals achieved a great deal politically in the eighties, they could have accomplished much, much more. One reason they failed to fulfill their potential reverberates from God's eighth-century-B.C. indictment of Israel: "My people are destroyed from lack of knowledge" (Hosea 4:6).

Sometimes Christian ignorance about political matters hurts because "what we 'know' just isn't so." *Los Angeles Times* sportswriter, Jim Murray said it well, "We cling to myths, as hardy as dandelions." Just as it's difficult to rid the lawn of those perennial yellow flowers with their miserable broad leaves, demythologizing politics is tough. People are confident about what they believe—even when it is wrong. But if we are to be effective in the political arena, we must uproot the weeds of our mistaken notions or remain handicapped by misinformation.

MYTH #1: ALL POLITICIANS ARE CROOKS

Too many Americans willingly accept Mark Twain's observation that "It could probably be shown by facts that there is no distinctly native American criminal class except Congress." Years ago I would have laughed with everyone else at the old curmudgeon's cynicism. Not any more. I know too much.

This kind of widespread skepticism breeds distrust and, eventually, disdain for our system of government. It is a poisonous attitude. If the disrespect was generally deserved, that would be one thing—but it is not. As with mother-in-law jokes, a sense of fair play demands that we stop making political officeholders the object of ridicule.

My earliest forays into the world of politics taught me much. I had set out to get acquainted with my party's leaders and its most active workers in order to gain support for my run for Congress. Night after night I would come home and tell my wife, Lynne, about the truly fine people I had met. Frankly, I was surprised. I assumed I would be meeting power-hungry political operatives, but instead I encountered genuinely concerned people who wanted to improve our society. With an idealism tempered by realism, they were volunteers in the best sense of the word. High caliber people that they were, most expected nothing but the satisfaction that comes from a job well done.

My guess is that the same is true for most of the other party's workers. Of course, I don't mean to canonize them all. There are losers in the ranks, including persons with hidden political agendas or selfish ends in mind. The same goes for some elected officials. But as a rule, those I came to know were genuinely admirable people.

When I became Colorado's Senate chaplain I suddenly acquired dozens of political officeholders as acquaintances and, before long, friends. Here, too, I was surprised at what I found. The vast majority of them were dedicated public servants. The majority—not all.

Take one senator who had become a good friend. One morning I was dumbfounded to read in the papers that his management consultant business had gone belly up. After the invocation, I asked him to sit with me on the Senate floor. Wasn't there anything he could have done to save his business? "Sure, I could have saved it by resigning from the Senate and devoting my full attention to it," he said. Why hadn't he? "Because I consider serving in this body a sacred trust from the people who elected me."

In Colorado, the legislature held a long session every other year running nearly six months. Alternate years should have run three months, but often went four or more. Many senators had put their personal businesses on the back burner during these months, and I recall several Senate wives confiding how tough it was on their husbands to start over each year after adjournment. Even then, however, they remained on constant call from constituents and were frequently assigned heavy interim committee responsibilities. In those years, 1974-75, the senators were paid the princely sum of $7,600 per year.

I recall another senator taking three unpaid days of leave to argue a case in court. His client won a judgment of $70,000, which netted his law firm a 30 percent commission of $21,000. This lawyer was able to generate in three days almost three times his annual Senate salary. He certainly wasn't in the legislature for the money. Nor were most of the others.

There are other benefits for serving in public life: a sense of power or fulfillment, contacts that lead to opportunities, the chance to run for yet higher offices, and increased self-esteem, to mention a few. Admitting all that, most of these people are to be regarded as genuine public servants. The same goes for a good percentage of the members of Congress, or of your local school board or city council. The reality is that most elected bodies

probably contain dishonest or decent officials in direct proportion to the citizenry in the state, district, or community where
they serve.

Christians must be especially careful here. It is easy to violate the Lord's command: "Do not judge, or you will be judged.
For in the same way you judge others, you will be judged…"
(Matthew 7:1-2). We must have opinions in order to navigate
life, but the biblical word *judge* refers to condemning.

Suppose a friend says, "Look, I don't want to hear any more
about your Christian faith. As far as I'm concerned, all religion is
a racket and all preachers are Jimmy Swaggarts." It pains you that
your friend has so badly misjudged Christianity. Tragically, she is
dead wrong, and you want to protest.

Consider how it must feel to be an honest officeholder who
has the impression that you and your friends (suppose it is your
whole church!) think of him as crooked. You too could be dead
wrong, so don't judge.

MYTH #2: YOU CAN'T LEGISLATE MORALITY

The dogmatism of those who repeat this mantra would be
laughable, except that it is no laughing matter. Christians have
been beaten into political inactivity by the mindless repetition of
this line. They have been made to feel that they are out of
bounds, in foul territory, when they attempt, for example, to
protect unborn human life.

Sincere disciples of this dogma are very much like a bishop
of a century ago, who pronounced from his pulpit and in the
periodical he edited, that heavier-than-air flight was both impossible and contrary to the will of God. Oh, the irony that Bishop
Wright had two sons, Orville and Wilbur! Wright was wrong.
Sure of himself, but dead wrong.

Those who honestly oppose the idea of legislating morality are convinced that any such effort is futile. They will predictably contend, for example, that if abortion on demand is declared illegal, women will still have abortions—thereby proving that such moral behavior cannot be legislated.

But shall we then eradicate laws against stealing because millions will break them? Most Americans want society's standard to remain firm: Stealing is wrong. Whether some citizens make careers of burglarizing homes, stealing cars, or picking pockets is beside the point. The law sets the standard.

Others hide behind this myth for devious reasons. They resent the pressure for religion-based morality in society and wish to make pro-lifers feel guilty for forcing their personal moral convictions on others. Of course, they never admit that if their pro-abortion view prevails, that would be the "moral position" of our society under the law. Then they would be forcing *their* morality onto society.

Whatever happens, our society will have values. The only question is, what will they be? Cardinal John O'Connor of New York put his finger on the problem in his book *His Eminence and Hizzoner,* co-authored with former New York Mayor Ed Koch. "Public officials, perhaps more than most people, are fond of saying they have no right to impose their moral beliefs on others. That's equivalent to saying their obligation is to make only value-free judgments. That's nonsense. They would have to remain mute about all public policy issues. To make a value-free judgment is to make no judgment at all."[1]

Anyone still convinced that "you can't legislate morality" should turn to the civil rights movement of the sixties. Honest scholars and the media must acknowledge that the civil rights movement was driven by deep religious conviction—just as were the anti-slavery and abolitionist movements in the United States and England. What our nation conclusively legislated was this conviction: "All men [and women] are created equal." In this case not only did we legislate morality, we legislated theology. There's hypocrisy here. Some among the media and academic elite who applauded the moral influence of religion in the civil rights struggle of the sixties are the same people who denounce the moral influence of religion in the abortion battle of the eighties and nineties. In this case, they resist our "morality" because it differs from theirs.

But does that not pierce to the very nature of the democratic state? All laws are impositions on someone unless they are unanimously supported. Some Americans were not pleased when women were given the right to vote through ratification of the nineteenth Amendment in 1920. But the majority imposed its will on the minority, constitutionally enforcing the moral conviction that justice required that women be treated equally and no longer disenfranchised.

Not only can we legislate morality, we must! The simple fact is that Congress and our state legislatures do it every day. Speed limits on interstate highways and social security legislation both flow from tough decisions about the moral responsibility of government.

MYTH #3: IT IS IMPOSSIBLE FOR A CHRISTIAN TO SERVE IN POLITICS BECAUSE POLITICS REQUIRES COMPROMISE

My lunch with a prosperous business friend was fruitful. He was about to give me a $500 check for my congressional campaign, but he wasn't going to let go of it easily. There were some things he wanted to say. Expressing personal confidence in my integrity, he nevertheless worried that if I became a member of Congress, I would inevitably change—and not for the better. Like many others I would compromise here and there and be the worse for it. He feared that, spiritually, I would never be the same.

I had thought a lot about such concerns long before my friend ever raised them. I had firmly determined never to compromise my convictions. On the other hand, it seemed to me that a proper humility required that I be open to compromising my opinions. Who needs a congressman who thinks he has all the answers before going to Washington? Who needs a congresswoman for whom committee hearings, expert testimony, and thoughtful debate are irrelevant and a waste of time?

Compromise is not a bad word. Husbands and wives who have not learned to compromise have probably long since ceased living together. Shall we vacation at the beach or in the mountains? Shall we go to a basketball game or a concert tonight? Shall we buy *Encyclopedia Britannica* or a large-screen TV? Nobody has it his way all the time.

Likewise in politics. Let's just pick some numbers out of the air. Suppose I am a senator who is convinced that it will require $1 billion to help Rwanda's refugees adequately. Having argued for that amount, I realize that the most the Senate will appropriate and the president will sign is $500 million. Shall I vote against the smaller amount, preferring nothing to a "compromise" of my opinion? And what if my vote becomes the swing vote and no aid is then authorized? The applicable political adage is: "Half a loaf is better than none." If that's compromise, I have no problem with it. Those who don't hold the high office of dictator must settle for what they can get.

There's another kind of compromise, however, that is unthinkable for a Christian. Should I violate my deep convictions about the unique value of life made in the image of God to vote pro-choice if the polls showed that 75 percent of the people in my district favored abortion "rights"? God helping me, I would not make that kind of compromise even to get re-elected. Trading a birthright for a mess of pottage is never a good deal.

What I would have done as a member of Congress is purely theoretical because I never made it there. But for four fellow alumni of Wheaton College in Illinois, the situation is quite different.

Indiana's Dan Coats was the first to be elected, in 1980. Since 1988 he has been a member of the Senate. Then followed the late Paul Henry of Michigan in 1984, with Dennis Hastert of Illinois two years later. Politically very different from the three Republicans is liberal Democrat Jim McDermott of Washington, elected to the House in 1988. House Chaplain Jim Ford says it's unprecedented to have such a delegation in Congress from a school of only two thousand students—and an evangelical college at that.

This modest congressional chapter of the Wheaton Alumni Club would have been a great place to check the validity of the third myth. Are Christian members of Congress inevitably forced to compromise their convictions? I can hear them answer in unison: "No!"

MYTH #4: THERE'S NOT A DIME'S WORTH OF DIFFERENCE BETWEEN THE PARTIES

It was George Wallace in 1968, trying to justify his independent candidacy for president, who uttered the oft-quoted dictum: "There's not a dime's worth of difference between the parties." Maybe not on the civil rights issue, which was all-important to

Wallace that year, but the disparities between the parties have always been significant.

Over the years there have been hundreds of billions of dimes' worth of difference between them. One major difference is the constituencies to which the parties appeal. Since 1979 I've been at the table a good number of times as top Republican officials such as national chairmen Bill Brock, Lee Atwater, and Haley Barbour cultivated evangelical support. Through the platform-construction presidential election years of 1980, 1984, 1988, and 1992, as well as the alternating congressional election years, they kept asking how they could tailor their positions to appeal to evangelical voters' beliefs.

By contrast, I was excluded from the table of the Democratic policy-makers. That was not surprising. Any party which for years persisted in giving official recognition to a gay and lesbian caucus could hardly be construed as wooing evangelicals. In 1988, for example, Republicans invited NAE to testify before their national convention platform committee. When no similar invitation was forthcoming from the Democrats, we initiated contact with them. I was told there would be no equivalent opportunity for NAE to speak to their platform committee.

But this claim wasn't quite true. The opportunity was there, someone just didn't want our input. I testified before the Republicans in Kansas City on May 31, and several days later (unknown to us), the Democrat platform committee met in Columbus. The National Abortion Rights Action League received an invitation to provide input, but we did not.

When we first learned that evangelicals would be unable to appear before the Democrats, I inquired about submitting a written testimony. Without enthusiasm, my informant supposed it would be okay. "How many copies do you need and what is the deadline?" I asked. He thought two copies should do it. Two copies? He should have been fired for failing at least to pretend that his party was interested in our concerns. Nobody at the Democratic National Committee headquarters was going to remove my staple, duplicate our statement at their expense, and distribute it to all the members of its platform committee, much less offer copies to the media. Four years later, nothing had changed. In 1992 I flew, by invitation, to one platform committee hearing only. The GOP was meeting in Salt Lake City.

Back in 1984, the parties' divergence had become especially clear on the traditional major issues of peace and prosperity. Believing that weakness invites aggression, Ronald Reagan and the Republicans wanted to give military spending a larger share of the budget. The Democrats wanted to reduce the rate of increase in defense spending and would have ended production of two major weapons systems. Republicans supported and Democrats opposed the Strategic Defense Initiative. Reagan contended that the Mutual Assured Destruction stand-off lived up to its acronym, MAD, and that Mutual Assured Security through "star wars" was the truly moral course to take.

When it came to prosperity, Reagan's party said people must be given an equal opportunity to compete on the basis of merit, under equal protection of the law. To Walter Mondale's party, economic fairness required unusual treatment of individuals in order to produce greater equality of results. Tax policies and affirmative action illustrated these philosophically conflicting approaches. The rhetoric about a "conservative opportunity society" versus a "liberal welfare state" may have been overblown, but it focused the debate and delineated real differences between the two parties.

In 1988, everybody in America who could read lips knew which party was committed to no new taxes. In fact, his breaking that promise was so dismaying that it cost President Bush the enthusiasm of many in his party. It further raised questions of his integrity, which ultimately may have resulted in his failed bid for re-election in 1992.

Here are some other issues, lifted from the official party platforms on which George Bush and Michael Dukakis ran for president. They further reveal the vast differences between the two parties.

Democrats opposed the federal death penalty and supported gun control; the GOP took the other side on both issues. Republicans supported a human life amendment to protect the unborn and opposed federal funding of abortions; Democrats wanted to guarantee the fundamental right of reproductive choice and insisted on federal funding of abortions. Democrats supported a federally regulated child care system and opposed any religious activity even in church-run centers; the GOP supported a tax-credit approach, which would not discriminate against mothers staying at home or religious day-care centers. Both parties supported equal pay for equal work, but Republicans opposed and Democrats supported passage of the Equal Rights Amendment.

Democrats prefer an activist, sharply expanding government. Republicans have an opposing commitment to individual liberty and limited government. In 1994, Republican chairman Haley Barbour put it bluntly: "We are the conservative party." South Carolina Governor Carroll Campbell reinforced his chairman: The GOP "is the party that, on a two-lane highway, drives down the right-hand side of the road." When your friends want to argue that the differences between the parties are only inconsequential, tell them to look again.

MYTH #5: I'M ONLY ONE PERSON—ONE PERSON WOULDN'T MAKE ANY DIFFERENCE

Sue Myrick, elected to Congress in 1994 but Charlotte, North Carolina's mayor at the time, was addressing the final breakfast meeting of NAE's Federal Seminar for Christian collegians. Her comments were forceful and on target. Suddenly she shifted gears: "How many Polish people..." she began. For a split second my mind raced. *She wouldn't be about to tell an ethnic joke, would she? Of course not; she's not that kind of person, and besides, she's too intelligent to destroy her career with that kind of humor.* Her voice penetrated my runaway thoughts and I heard her complete the question: "How many Polish people does it take to turn the world around?... One—if his name is Lech Walesa."

What a beautiful twist. The frequently maligned Polish people received a magnificent compliment. One of their shipyard workers becomes an independent trade union leader whose courage and humble effectiveness results in his country's first free election in forty years, and the installation of the first Eastern bloc non-Communist prime minister in decades. That one man helped change the course of Eastern European history.

But let's move back to American politics. In the summer of 1983, Pennsylvania teenager Lisa Bender struck a giant blow for the cause of religious liberty in the United States. As a high school student in Williamsport, Lisa wanted to begin a prayer club. When officials refused her that right, she took them to court. With the help of Sam Ericsson and the Christian Legal Society, she won. Her victory in court then prompted legislators to draw up and secure passage of the Equal Access Act.

The lesson is simple. One high school student, faithful to her convictions, moved Congress to act. In a similar situation, Bridget Mergens of Omaha, Nebraska, ultimately forced the Supreme Court to vindicate her religious free speech rights by ruling that public high schools must treat all noncurriculum related student groups alike. Lisa and Bridget. Two high school girls. Acting one at a time.

When the proposed Equal Rights Amendment was sent from Congress to the states for ratification, it appeared headed for quick adoption into the Constitution. But that never happened, even though three presidents, Congress, both parties at that time, the labor movement, and the national media supported the ERA. As one state legislature after another got on the bandwagon, one person who thought through the implications of this far-reaching amendment decided to act. Phyllis Schlafly singlehandedly stopped the ERA on its fast track. An attorney and outstanding debater, this wife and mother of six would deny that she did it alone, but she was the one to organize tens of thousands of volunteers into the Stop ERA movement. One person can make the difference.

Here's a name few readers will recognize—today. Wait a few years. Joe Watkins was a young black preacher who volunteered to work in two Indiana campaigns in 1980, Dan Quayle's for the Senate and Dan Coats' for Congress. Both won. Early in 1989, Watkins became an associate director of the Office of Public Liaison in George Bush's White House. Who can predict what influence Joe will eventually have?

Several times I've had the privilege of preaching at Calvary Temple in Denver. I particularly recall a Sunday morning in February 1982 when I had tried to build a case for Christian political involvement. When I was done, Pastor Charles Blair rose and said he was ashamed to admit it, but he had never attended a precinct caucus in all his years in Colorado. He promised to do so that year and urged all his people to do likewise.

Now, jump to Denver's McNichols Arena early that summer, where Republicans were meeting for their state convention. I had barely started down the aisle leading to my Jefferson County delegation, when a woman spotted me from below. She charged up the steps toward me, calling, "You're Bob Dugan, aren't you? I heard you speak at Calvary Temple last winter, and when Pastor Blair said he was going to his caucus I made up my mind to attend mine. Now look. I hardly knew what to do there, but I was elected to the county, congressional, and state conventions. So here I am today, with a voice in determining the person we will nominate for governor." She saw herself playing an important role. She was right.

One person's vote can make a massive difference as well. In the early 1800s, an Indiana farmer named Henry Shoemaker formed a ballot from a paper bag when his polling place had run out of ballots. He cast his vote for Madison Marsh for state representative; Marsh won by one vote. In those days, state legislatures elected U.S. senators, so Marsh voted for a man named Harrigan to represent Indiana in the Senate. Harrigan won by one vote. In the Senate, Harrigan cast his roll call vote in favor of Texas' bid for statehood. Texas became a state by a margin of one single vote.

In 1994 Senate minority leader Bob Dole made it a habit to stress the importance of a single vote in Congress. "We passed a $260 billion tax increase last year by one vote in the House and one vote in the Senate." No exaggeration. It's true. So, going into November's elections, more than two hundred House challengers were each able to say, truthfully, that the incumbent they were seeking to unseat had cast the deciding vote for higher taxes.

Let's agree to throw out the cliché about one person never making a difference. And don't assume that you could never be an international figure like Lech Walesa. Before Solidarity he was an electrician in the Gdansk shipyards.

MYTH #6: PREACHERS SHOULD STAY OUT OF POLITICS

I once bought this platitude hook, line, and sinker. As far as I knew, nobody in my boyhood congregation of one thousand ever ran for political office or helped someone who did—least of all the pastor. Politics occasionally drew a pronouncement from the pulpit, but generally only with resentment or sarcasm. Moreover, nothing gleaned in college or seminary days would have inclined me to dirty my hands in politics. Today I believe the reverse.

Ordained ministers cannot be deprived of their rights as citizens. Tennessee once had a law prohibiting clergy from running for public office. In 1977, in *McDaniel v. Paty*, the Supreme Court struck down that law, Justice William J. Brennan writing:

> Government may not inquire into the religious beliefs and motivations of officeholders—it may not remove them from office merely for making public statements regarding religion, nor question whether their legislative actions stem from religious conviction.[2]

I am not urging pastors to resign their churches and run for Congress. On the other hand, running for a part-time position on the school board might be something readily pursued.

Most ministers and church boards worry about jeopardizing their church's tax-exempt status if they become involved in politics. Such a fear has rendered many churches politically impotent. The first thing to be done, then, is for pastors to learn exactly what is allowable and what is not. For that purpose, a full legal analysis titled "Political Activity by Clergymen" is included as an appendix to this book.

Two positive words set the tone. First, neither the Internal Revenue Service nor the Federal Election Commission has ever interfered with a church's right to educate its people on moral or political issues. Second, we know of no case where a clergyman has been questioned for endorsing or opposing a candidate, even from the pulpit, as long as it is only his personal view. Whether that is prudent or advisable, however, is a different question.

Churches can hold nonpartisan voter registration drives or political forums as long as all candidates are invited. Educational materials about candidates' views on issues, voting records, and the like may be distributed, as long as they comply with IRS rules on neutrality. Candidates may be introduced in a service, or even pray or speak, but not ask for money. Churches may contribute to a legislative, moral, or educational issue campaign, although they may not spend a "substantial" part of their activity in so doing.[3] Churches cannot establish a political action committee (PAC) or contribute funds to a candidate or political party.

Incidentally, in his "Super Sunday Campaign" in 1988, the Reverend Jesse Jackson solicited contributions from hundreds of churches, in what appeared to be a blatant violation of IRS regulations. The IRS did not interfere. (One wonders if the media would have stood silently by if then-presidential candidate Pat Robertson had done the same thing.) The fact is that in our history as a nation, no church has yet lost its tax-exempt status with the IRS for being "too political." None. Zero.

As for ministers themselves, they may support candidates or preach about issues while identified as pastors of their churches. They may lobby as individuals and they most assuredly may preach about the importance of political involvement or publicly pray about elections. Again, a pastor's personal or public support of any candidate will not endanger his church's tax-exempt status, although, for a number of reasons, he would be well advised not to make a regular practice of doing so.

Should pastors get involved in politics? Of course. If they do not, few of their people are likely to do so, and Christian "salt" will not get poured out of the church's shaker into a society that desperately needs the preservative. Salt must come in contact with that which it would preserve.

MYTH #7: YOU CAN'T FIGHT CITY HALL

Of the myths I have listed, this should be the easiest to discredit. For Christians, a one-sentence reminder that "with God all things are possible" should do it (Matthew 19:26; Mark 9:23, Luke 18:27).

Beyond that it is easy to point to instances where city hall was roundly defeated. Look at San Francisco's city hall in early July 1989, where Mayor Art Agnos was poised to sign the Domestic Partners Ordinance passed by the Board of Supervisors. On the day before he would sign, a group of concerned citizens presented petitions with over twenty-seven thousand signatures that temporarily put the ordinance on hold until the citizens of San Francisco could express themselves in a November ballot referendum.

The ordinance would have permitted unmarried couples to register their partnerships, much like traditional couples filing marriage licenses. That in turn would have resulted in health and life insurance benefits heretofore available only to married couples. The ordinance was regarded by the gay and lesbian community in San Francisco as a landmark for civic acceptance of gays, a model ordinance for other cities. But the petitions caught city hall by surprise.

The results in November's balloting were even more stunning. The temporary roadblock that forced Mayor Agnos to put the cap back on his pen became a permanent barrier. The voters turned down the Domestic Partners Ordinance in the American city with the largest and most politically formidable homosexual bloc. This battle, part of the gay agenda to legitimize homosexuality as an acceptable lifestyle, was over for now.

The victory came only after a few concerned evangelicals discovered that Roman Catholic leaders were as troubled about the ordinance as they were. As the churches began to pray, they sought national prayer support for their strategic fight. San Francisco churches cooperated in an unprecedented fashion, first to secure petition signatures, then to organize—with professional guidance—to defeat the ordinance. It was a remarkable and gratifying achievement.[4]

Be assured that you can not only fight city hall, but state legislatures and Congress as well. There was a forerunner to the San Francisco confrontation, which then state assemblyman Art Agnos was involved in as well. In 1984, he led the California legislature to adopt gay rights legislation. Evangelicals were not organized adequately to defeat the bill, but afterward they provided strong and compelling moral support that emboldened Governor George Deukmejian to veto it.

When evangelicals fought city hall in San Francisco, they won a victory for traditional moral values, thus strengthening the entire nation. What if they had believed the myth?

That brings up a sobering question: How many victories are slipping away each day simply because too many among us "know" what just isn't so? It's time to shelve these myths permanently—for the good of our nation and for the preservation of a national heritage worth passing on.

WHAT

THE

BIBLE

COMMANDS

Chapter Three

DOES GOD WANT CHRISTIANS INVOLVED IN POLITICS?

ᔕᘉ

As evangelical Christians we are committed to the absolute authority and trustworthiness of the Bible for belief and behavior. Understanding how Jesus Christ regards the Scriptures, our minds are convinced and our wills are bound.

Jesus' view is wrapped up in one text: "The Scripture cannot be broken" (John 10:35). Each of the three times the Devil tempted Jesus in the desert, Jesus replied, "It is written..." (See Matthew 4, Mark 1, Luke 4), followed by a quotation from the Torah. His meaning was clear: Since it is written, the issue is settled. "I tell you the truth, until heaven and earth disappear, not the smallest letter, not the least stroke of a pen, will by any means disappear from the Law until everything is accomplished" (Matthew 5:18).

If the Bible commanded, "Thou shalt not engage in politics," most evangelicals wouldn't touch politics with a ten-foot pole. On the other hand, there is no eleventh commandment that says "Thou shalt vote." I suspect that, if asked, many evangelical Christians couldn't answer confidently what the Bible says about political involvement. If they ventured an opinion, they would probably be unable to cite biblical support for it.

The Bible does offer clear principles regarding believers and politics. Let me rest my case on one of many passages, an incident recorded in Luke's Gospel:

> The teachers of the law and the chief priests looked for a way to arrest him immediately, because they knew he had spoken this parable against them. But they were afraid of the people.
>
> Keeping a close watch on him, they sent spies, who pretended to be honest. They hoped to catch Jesus in something he said so that they might hand him over to the power and authority of the governor. So the spies questioned him: "Teacher, we know that you speak and teach what is right, and that you do not show partiality but teach the way of God in accordance with the truth. Is it right for us to pay taxes to Caesar or not?
>
> He saw through their duplicity and said to them, "Show me a denarius. Whose portrait and inscription are on it?"
>
> "Caesar's," they replied.
>
> He said to them, "Then give to Caesar what is Caesar's, and to God what is God's."

They were unable to trap him in what he
had said there in public. And astonished by his
answer, they became silent (Luke 20:19-26).

Without vandalizing the text, I want to lift from it two clear
biblical principles that are universally applicable to Christians
and politics. In King James phraseology, these axioms are:
"Render to Caesar what is Caesar's" and "Render to God what is
God's." Since God merits the top line, let's consider our responsibility to him first.

RENDERING TO GOD

Since the Bible is its own best interpreter, the Apostle Paul's first
letter to a young pastor named Timothy is instructive:

I urge, then, first of all, that requests, prayers,
intercession and thanksgiving be made for
everyone—for kings and all those in authority,
that we may live peaceful and quiet lives in
all godliness and holiness. This is good, and
pleases God our Savior, who wants all men to
be saved and to come to a knowledge of the
truth (1 Timothy 2:1-4).

Translating "kings" into our political terminology, it could
not be more obvious that God expects his people to pray for
their leaders. Regarding our role as citizens in the world, *intelligent intercession for politicians* is our first responsibility—what it
takes to "render to God what is God's." To intercede meaning-
fully for all 435 representatives and for the one hundred senators

would be impossible. Who could remember even half of their names, or know enough about them to intercede effectively?

Surely the Lord does not expect Christians who live in Colorado to pray regularly for the senators who represent New Mexico, Virginia, or Vermont. But Colorado's two senators are theirs, elected to represent them. God does expect Coloradan Christians to pray for their senators just as he expects true Christians in every state to pray for those whom they have put in office. If we don't pray for our elected officials we are being disobedient to the direct instruction of Scripture. Praying for public officials is not optional for the Christian.

Who else should be on the prayer list? A minimum of seven elected officials represents every citizen in national and state government. It makes a good starting list, one for each day of the week. Prayer for the president can be expanded to include his vice president, his cabinet, and his senior advisors. The Supreme Court can be added at any time, as can the mayor and city council and school board in your home town.

I revealed my basic seven at the baccalaureate service at Roberts Wesleyan College in late spring 1990. Not wanting to embarrass the faculty and administration seated in the choir loft behind me, I excused them from participating. Then I asked everyone else to stand. "I am putting you on your honor," I said. "When I mention a political position for which you have a prayer responsibility, silently determine if you know that official's name. If not, please be seated."

I began with the president. Happily, no one sat down. "Your state's governor," I continued. Believe it or not, more than several dozen slid into their pews. Casualties mounted when I mentioned "one U.S. senator from your state," and multiplied with "the other Senator from your state." After "the Congressperson who represents your district," only 25 percent of the audience was still standing. Had I named the sixth and seventh who should have been on that prayer list—their state senator and state representative—not more than one in twenty would have remained on their feet.

It doesn't take Sherlock Holmes to arrive at some revealing conclusions from this demonstration. If Christian people do not know the names of those whom they have elected, it follows that they have not been interceding for them—and that they are disobeying their Lord.

One more powerful point needed to be made with the three hundred left from our original twelve hundred. To those still on their feet, I said softly, "If you have not prayed for your president, your governor, your two senators, and your representative at least once since the beginning of this year, by name, please be seated with the others." Of the twelve hundred present only one man remained standing.

Who can imagine what God might do in response to the knowledgeable intercession of millions of evangelicals for their elected officials? I mean *intelligent* intercession. If it is not meaningless to pray, "Lord, bless everybody in our family, Amen," or "Help all the missionaries supported by our church," then "Bless all the politicians, Amen," is no better.

We need to start reading the newspapers with renewed interest to see how "our" politicians are voting. We will want to hear them speak, perhaps at town meetings where we can meet them and watch them handle tough questions. We may be pleasantly surprised at how close we can get to them, and we'll develop opinions about their personal character and their value systems. Surely we will want to know about their families and even hope to discover whether they share our faith. Paul says that the

ultimate end of our prayers is that all would "be saved and come
to the knowledge of the truth."

Intercessory prayer for our political officeholders is a clear
responsibility that Christians have overlooked—to the detriment
of the nation. But it's also an oversight that can be corrected. The
"God who is there," to use Francis Schaeffer's memorable phrase,
hears and answers our prayers.

RENDERING TO CAESAR

How we "render to Caesar what is Caesar's" depends on how we
identify America's equivalent of the Roman emperor. Caesar, of
course, was the final, unchallenged political authority in the New
Testament era. We can eliminate the president, then, for his veto
can be overridden by the House and Senate. Congress is assuredly
not Caesar, because the Supreme Court can rule its laws unconstitutional. Nor is the Supreme Court Caesar, perhaps to your
surprise, for Congress can make exceptions and regulations to its
appellate jurisdiction.

Only one "Caesar" remains, and "he" is none of the above.
Our Caesar is the Constitution. This, our final political authority,
defines and controls the separated powers among the legislative,
executive, and judicial branches of our government.

We are part of the marvelous social contract expressed by the
Constitution's Preamble:

> We the People of the United States, in Order to
> form a more perfect Union, establish Justice,
> insure domestic Tranquility, provide for the
> common defence, promote the general Welfare,
> and secure the Blessings of Liberty to ourselves

and our Posterity, do ordain and establish this
Constitution for the United States of America.

In the next few lines, the Constitution quite clearly spells out
what our "Caesar" expects. Article I, Section 2, just four lines
into the body of the document, says: "The House of
Representatives shall be composed of Members chosen every second Year by the People of the several States." Section 3 was
amended in 1913 so that the people, rather than the legislature,
would directly elect their senators, and Article II outlines the
people's responsibility for electing the president.

Our Lord expects that the normal pattern of Christian living
will find his followers giving to Caesar what belongs to Caesar.
Since there is no other way to put leaders into office in a democratic republic than for the people to choose them, we must be
involved. Naturally, we would not wish to offend God by doing
so irresponsibly, nor would we want to fail our nation by doing
so ignorantly. That is why I add a crucial adjective as I define our
second biblical duty as *informed involvement in politics*.

Let me make a vital distinction here. Our Christian politics
will be more effective and less objectionable if we emphasize individual involvement, rather than institutional involvement. In
other words, the church should not try to move politically as a
church, but its activity will be the sum total of the participation of
all its members. No one can reasonably object to that pattern, not
even the *Washington Post* or an Internal Revenue Service lawyer.

What kind of mobilization would make evangelical congre-
gations a force for righteousness in their communities and in the
nation? Imagine all of their members politically active at the
minimal level, a tenth of their members at the maximum level,
and one-fourth of their people at a moderate level.

ONE HUNDRED PERCENT ACTIVE AT A
MINIMUM LEVEL—VOTING POLITICS

It would be hard to argue that anything less than being registered and voting knowledgeably would satisfy the minimum, basic demand of Christian citizenship. Ideally the church would publicize registration deadlines, hold nonpartisan voter registration drives in the church (possible in most places), and provide transportation to the polls for those who need it on Election Day.

Unfortunately, there's some quirky thinking out there that sometimes gets into the heads of evangelicals. On the Sunday after I lost my election, we were worshiping in a large Denver church. As the first note of the organ postlude sounded, a woman gripped my elbow. "You don't know me, but I know you," she said earnestly. "It's just terrible that you lost on Tuesday. We need men like you in Washington." She complimented me for a minute, making a strong case for my candidacy. Then, lowering her voice and turning toward Lynne, she confessed, "Of course, I didn't get out and vote for him. But I guess that didn't make any difference after all."

Apparently because I lost by more than one vote, she freely excused herself. Could she not reckon that if the votes of all my supporters who failed to cast a ballot had been added together, the outcome might have been different? Why do people think that way?

TEN PERCENT ACTIVE
AT A MAXIMUM LEVEL—PARTY POLITICS

By maximum political participation, I do not refer to elected officials or to people who earn their living as strategists or party staffers. I mean rather those volunteers who accept the responsibility of working in the party of their choice. Many will serve as precinct committeemen and women whose ultimate job is to deliver the vote in their precinct on Election Day. Others will be officers in county, state, or local party organizations.

Not a huge amount of time is required of the party's foot soldiers, but a willingness to work beyond the call of duty will lead to recognition and promotion. Cream always rises to the top. By virtue of their effectiveness, cooperative spirit, and dependability, some members of the party will inevitably move toward leadership. A few, who may have discovered an aptitude and liking for politics they didn't know they had, will eventually become candidates—supported by their fellow party workers.

One great advantage to having 10 percent of the church's members involved in the political parties is that they become a marvelous source of information about candidates and issues for the 90 percent who are doing other things. Their enthusiasm will create ample interest to guarantee a high-percentage voter turnout among their brothers and sisters in the church.

TWENTY-FIVE PERCENT ACTIVE
AT A MODERATE LEVEL—CAMPAIGN POLITICS

Not only will the party activists inspire voter interest, but they will also recruit friends from the church to help in campaigns. Each would only need to enlist one or two persons to boost her church to the point where 25 percent are walking the precincts with literature on a couple of evenings or Saturday mornings or giving other tangible help. Some will host a neighborhood coffee where their circle of friends can meet a candidate personally. Others will give volunteer hours in the campaign office, help get out a newsletter or fund-raising mailing, or make calls from the telephone bank. In addition, it would be a tremendous boost if each could contribute even a modest check to the campaign.

Take it from the professionals. These campaign volunteers, recruited by the most dedicated workers, are the people who determine the outcome of an election. Former White House aide Morton Blackwell, a developer and trainer of conservative political activists, correctly insists that campaigns are not so much contests between Candidate A and Candidate B, or between Party D and Party R, as they are skirmishes and full-blown battles between the activists supporting A and those supporting B.

The Friday before Election Day in 1976, a first-time volunteer showed up at our campaign headquarters, wanting to go door-to-door for me. She confided that for months she had intended to give me a hand but had procrastinated. She didn't know where to phone to volunteer, and she was apprehensive about whether she would take to walking precincts, or quite possibly hate it. Would she have a bunch of doors slammed in her face? It was time to put her anxieties behind her. "If I don't help you this weekend, it will be too late."

When our group gathered for lunch, she was excited. She had loved the contact with people and felt she was making a difference for me. Indeed she was. Undoubtedly there were hundreds who could have done what she did, including most of my committee of three hundred, each of whom could have been involved a handful more. Imagine more than a thousand folks going door-to-door over a couple of weekends. I would have won in a walk.

Under any form of government, a Christian's first political assignment is *intelligent intercession for politicians*. Under our form of government, their second political responsibility is *informed involvement in politics*. If our churches resembled the ideal I have sketched above, we evangelicals could be a force for the kind of righteousness that "exalts a nation" and against the sin that is "a disgrace to any people" (Proverbs 14:34).

Scripture affirms, and experience attests, that God works primarily through the Body of Christ—the Church—to accomplish his objectives in the world. Even a cursory reading of the Old Testament will reveal how often he achieved his objectives through kings, lawmakers, or judges. Only a fool would assert that God has no interest in presidential elections, congressional legislation, or Supreme Court decisions in the United States in the final decade of the twentieth century. Spiritually astute followers of Christ ought to be thinking through questions about how God may want to use the Body of Christ to accomplish his purposes through politics.

THE PASTOR'S ROLE

Pivotal to the effectiveness of any church is the shepherd—the pastor—who serves under the authority of the Chief Shepherd, and who must, as the Apostle Peter argues, be an example to the flock (1 Peter 5:1-4). If the spiritual leader does not encourage (good), or empower (better), or enable (best) his people to take an active role in politics, that church may well become culturally irrelevant.

Of course I know full well that any church that preaches God's truth, even if it confines its activity within the church's walls, cannot be totally irrelevant. Spiritually needy people may find their way in and even be introduced to Christ. But other churches will have to carry the battle to protect that church's religious freedom, to provide the best government possible, and to preserve the nation's morality.

Politicians tend to give evangelical pastors more credence than the pastors give themselves. They aptly perceive pastors as community leaders with considerable spheres of influence. Those who preach to three thousand on any Sunday may seem more important to them than those with one hundred in their congregation, but the smaller church is not to be ignored.

Having been a pastor for eighteen years, I would like to suggest three functions for which pastors are answerable:

• A Prophetic Role as Expositor of the Scripture

In the Old Testament era, priests spoke to God on the people's behalf, while prophets spoke to the people on God's behalf. Even today, when pastors faithfully proclaim the Word of God, the collective weight of their proclamation can change a nation's thinking.

In his first formal debate with Stephen Douglas, Abraham Lincoln said: "In this and like communities, public sentiment is everything. With public sentiment, nothing can fail; without it, nothing can succeed. Consequently, he who molds public sentiment goes deeper than he who enacts statutes or pronounces [judicial] decisions. He makes statutes and decisions possible or impossible to be executed."[1]

It stands to reason that preachers must be well informed before they can be informative. An informed prophet must read a daily major city newspaper and at least one national news magazine weekly. He makes a fateful mistake if he secures all his news from the electronic media which, by their time constraints, if not ideological bias, pre-select what he will see or hear. Having a reliable source for timely information is crucial to the evangelical community he serves.

Early in this century, pastors and teachers were respected as the best–educated leaders in their communities. In those pre-television days, people thronged to large Sunday evening services to hear words of wisdom relating the Bible to the times. Today we must earn our hearing. The public is skeptical about religious leaders. Sheer hard work in the study is a necessity if our preaching is to be credible and compelling.

Informed pastors will do extensive reading in order to understand historic and religious currents. They must become like the "men of Issachar, who understood the times and knew what Israel should do" (1 Chronicles 12:32). Furthermore, they need to understand the political process, periodically reread the Constitution, and cut through to the correct meaning of separation of church and state. Pastors should be able to describe the nominating process in their states, with a rough schedule of dates and events, and be able to tell a member of the church how to get started in politics.

Some pastors will object to such demands upon their time, pleading that they only have time to study the Bible. I commend to them the model of the National Association of Evangelical's first president, Harold John Ockenga. His knowledge of history and of current events fleshed out his biblical preaching and invariably made him relevant, so that his Park Street Church pulpit in Boston was respected more than any in New England. How was that possible? Ockenga would frequently explain that preaching was his highest priority, his unique responsibility in the church. Other duties, however important, would have to be assigned to others if they interfered with adequate preparation to preach.

Evangelical preachers who limit their content to a personal, internalized, vertically-oriented message are guilty of shrinking the Bible. God's Word must be related to justice, to conscience, to societal values, to ideological conflicts. Pastoral prayers should reflect awareness and concern about issues and leaders. In the course of evangelizing and expounding the Scriptures, our pastors will be announcing the criteria by which God will judge the world—including the United States. Christians must calculate how those criteria affect their citizenship duties.

• A Pastoral Role as Equipper of the Believers

Evangelical preaching is too often long on what people ought to do but short on explaining how. Pastors convinced that Christians are bound by political responsibilities should naturally want to show them how to fulfill those duties.

Equipping them for prayer begins by modeling intercession for the president, the governor, and others by name, referring to some situation they face, in Sunday worship pastoral prayers. Beyond that, be creative. Once a month, those who wish could skip dinner and come an hour early for prayer meeting to fast and pray for their government and its leaders. People could be assigned, one per week, to prepare background information on a political officeholder, "introducing" him or her to a Sunday school class for a period of focused group prayer. A bulletin board with pictures of the congregation's political leaders would serve as a great prayer reminder, balancing the church's missionary map on the other wall.

Why have we allowed our members to feel powerless about politics when they could have been tapping the ultimate source of power through specific prayer? I wish I knew.

Larger churches could do it alone, or several evangelical churches in the community could cooperate in a Saturday prayer breakfast with their mayor, a state legislator, or their member of Congress as honored guest. One note of caution: Do not preach an evangelistic sermon to a conspicuous political audience of one. That would be using an otherwise good-faith invitation and unchristianly embarrassing your guest. Evangelism can come later, one-on-one, in conversation between friends. Let the office-holder speak; have questions and answers—never posed angrily or threateningly, but graciously and firmly. Inquire about family, personal and political concerns, and let the prayer time be an affirming and supportive experience for your guest. You will have built a relationship leading to friendship, and your people will know a great deal more about one of their leaders. That will allow them to pray and vote more wisely.

Equipping for participation may involve special candidate forums to which all candidates are invited. More than ten years ago, the evangelical churches on Staten Island, New York, hosted such an event. More than three hundred people stayed for over two hours, and the dozen candidates were so impressed that they talked about that Saturday night as being the real beginning of the campaign.

The pastor can announce voter registration deadlines and, as mentioned earlier, even hold a nonpartisan registration drive in the church. He may be enthused about building the case for evangelical political involvement through a sermon, or think it wise to invite a guest speaker for that purpose. Special seminars could teach church members the political ropes, always in a non-partisan way. Aim for the goals suggested above: 100 percent involved at the minimum level of voting politics, 10 percent at the maximum level of party politics, and 25 percent at the moderate level of campaign politics.

Every church should have a Christian Citizenship Ministry within its overall mission, through a governmental affairs or social concerns committee.[2] Additionally, a number of churches in a community or state could combine to produce educational materials for their churches, whether issues-analysis or candidate questionnaires. Get some good advice if you do. Asking candidates if they are born-again Christians, for example, can create resentment and provoke a backlash that will have the opposite effect from the helpful one you intend.

• A Personal Role as Example of the Believers

Sermons about political activity by pastors who are politically lethargic will fall on deaf ears. Who would buy a miracle hairgrowth restorer from a bald barber? To the extent that preachers or other deeply committed religious people stay out of politics, our government is less representative than it was designed to be. Like pastor, like people.

If pastors wish to go beyond the bare minimum of voting responsibly, they will need to get active in party politics and in campaign politics. Thinking pastors will set an example by resisting the lure of registering as independents. It is foolish to smugly announce that one is above the fray: "I just vote for the person, not for the party." That may sound good, but it's unconvincing. Independents take themselves straight out of the process by which the candidates are chosen and thus greatly reduce their influence on the eventual outcome. They simply stand aside and wait, hoping against hope that one party or the other will produce a worthwhile nominee.

Of course, there is no perfect political party. Neither is there a perfect church, a perfect husband, or a perfect pastor. In this imperfect world, choose the party closest to your way of thinking. Volunteer. Go as the Lord did, as a servant. With that kind of attitude, the party will welcome you with open arms—in much the same way that you are thrilled to have a new family come into your church, already committed to the Lord and eager to get to work. How many of those do you send away with "no" for an answer?

Pastors active in a political party will exemplify to their people that that's where the action is. They may also worry about dividing their congregation, but nothing of the kind is necessary. I think of three pastors in particular who became committeemen in my party in 1976 when I ran for Congress. They remained in their posts after my loss, and none created problems in his congregation.

One can be active in campaigns without hurting the spiritual unity of the church. People of both parties must genuinely be encouraged to labor in the political power structures. Neither by clever humor, innuendo, nor by partisan sermons should a pastor ever imply that his political position is the only option for his congregation. As wrong as it would be to shape a church so that only the rich would be attracted, it would equally be wrong to shape it so that only Republicans would feel comfortable there.

One Sunday evening I spoke in a fine church in a community north of New York City along the Hudson River. Afterward, a lovely couple expressed great delight that I had urged Christians to become politically involved. They had heard no such urging in the thirty years they had been members of the church.

They had a personal reason for hoping things would change. Their son, a lawyer and committed Christian, against great odds, had won a seat in the state assembly in Albany. He was reelected with 70 percent of the vote but now was running for another post at his party's strong urging. They thought he was the only one who could win it. Sadly, nobody in the church would help in his campaign, nor had anybody done so in the prior two campaigns. In fact, his mother reported that when she sought volunteers from among her friends she would often get a disdainful smile and the pious assurance that she need not worry, for "if the Lord wants him there, the Lord will put him there."

"Is that the way your church feels about evangelism and world missions?" I asked. "Do they suggest that if the Lord wants to convert people here or around the world, he'll take care of it? That there's no need to give sacrificially or to send the church's finest youth to the mission field?" Hardly.

This is a glaring inconsistency all too common in the Church today. When it comes to politics, we often behave as if God acts alone to put his candidates into office. But when it comes to evangelism, God suddenly becomes unable to accomplish his purposes without the sacrificial cooperation of the congregation.

We must not tolerate this illogical, contradictory, unbiblical thinking in the Church. If we do, our nation is in deep trouble.

Chapter Four

WHAT DOES JESUS ESPECIALLY WANT TO TEACH US?

To what kind of a political system do you owe your primary allegiance? "A Democracy!" you answer. I hope not. "Oh," you say, remembering the distinction reflected in the pledge of allegiance, "a Republic!" But this answer isn't quite right for the Christian either—not if you take Jesus seriously. The correct answer? A Monarchy. Did Jesus not command us to "seek first the kingdom of God and his righteousness, and all these things will be given to you as well" (Matthew 6:33)?

Perhaps the question is a bit tricky. But too few Christians, who take pride in being "people of the Book," would get the answer right. Pastors often find it easier to preach from the New Testament epistles of Paul, Peter, and the others, than from Jesus himself in the gospels. Or, when they do preach through a gospel, for some reason it is much more likely to be John's, rather than the other three.

That may explain why the major theme of Jesus' teachings, the kingdom of God, has been so overlooked. It is the principal theme in the first three books of the New Testament, the

Gospels according to Matthew, Mark, and Luke. Why, then, does this dominant doctrine of the kingdom of God remain a mystery to the people in our pews?

The obscurity that surrounds this doctrine may explain why evangelicals find it difficult to be rock-solid certain that their Lord wants them involved in transforming their culture through politics. This chapter is unique in this book. It's a Bible study on this major theme of Jesus' teachings—the kingdom of God.

The word *kingdom* is found ninety-eight times in the combined sixty-eight chapters of the first three gospels, but only five times in John. Is it right that we should last learn what Jesus first taught? "After John was put in prison, Jesus went into Galilee, proclaiming the good news of God. 'The time has come,' he said. 'The kingdom of God is near. Repent and believe the good news!'" (Mark 1:14-15). The kingdom of God was Jesus' first theme but it was also his final theme. "After his suffering, he showed himself to these men and gave many convincing proofs that he was alive. He appeared to them over a period of forty days and spoke about the kingdom of God" (Acts 1:3).

Most of us are aware that, as a missionary, the Apostle Paul preached the gospel throughout the Roman empire. Yet he fully grasped Jesus' kingdom teaching, revealing it in his summary of three years of ministry at Ephesus. "Now I know that none of you among whom I have gone about preaching the kingdom will ever see me again. Therefore, I declare to you today that I am innocent of the blood of all men. For I have not hesitated to proclaim to you the whole will of God" (Acts 20:25-27). At the end of his life, "For two whole years Paul stayed there [in Rome] in his own rented house and welcomed all who came to see him. Boldly and without hindrance he preached the kingdom of God and taught about the Lord Jesus Christ" (Acts 28:30-31).

Once we comprehend the implications of the kingdom of God, all uncertainties about the necessity of political involvement for the Christian will evaporate.

OUR IGNORANCE OF THE KINGDOM

As we set out to explore the subject of the kingdom of God, we have a handy scapegoat. We can blame the theologians. Over the twentieth century, European thinkers have sent mixed signals to the seminaries where pastors are trained.[1]

The kingdom is entirely *present*, according to Albrecht Ritschl, "the organization of humanity inspired by love."[2] He contended that futuristic terminology must be peeled from the doctrine like the husk from an ear of corn. Indeed, a religious magazine was renamed *The Christian Century* in 1900, in hopes that the century would see humanity organized by love, bringing in the kingdom.

The kingdom is entirely *future*, according to Albert Schweitzer. One can only hope that his worldwide renown as an organist and medical missionary were more deserved than his eminence as a theologian—a theologian who taught that Jesus was mistaken in expecting the kingdom in his lifetime.

It took a British theologian, C. H. Dodd, to teach that the kingdom is *both present and future*. The kingdom of God has come and is present, whether we know it or not, but it has a distinctly future aspect as well.

Why are there such differing views? They stem from a flawed approach to research—the fallacy of selective evidence. Pollsters wanting to know America's view on abortion rights cannot limit their questioning to members of the National Association of Evangelicals. Likewise, sampling only the mailing list of the National Organization for Women (NOW) would produce equally misleading statistics. To be trustworthy and valid, pollsters have a duty to report all opinions from scientifically selected random samplings.

And what is the biblical evidence? Obviously, the kingdom of God is *today,* a present reality:

> After John was put in prison, Jesus went into Galilee, proclaiming the good news of God. "The time has come," he said. "The kingdom of God is near. Repent and believe the good news" (Mark 1:14-15).

> But if I drive out demons by the Spirit of God, then the kingdom of God has come upon you (Matthew 12:28).

> The Law and the Prophets were proclaimed until John. Since that time, the good news of the kingdom of God is being preached, and everyone is forcing his way into it (Luke 16:16).

> Once, having been asked by the Pharisees when the kingdom of God would come, Jesus replied, "The kingdom of God does not come with your careful observation, nor will people say, 'Here it is,' or 'There it is,' because the kingdom of God is within you" (Luke 17:20-21).

> For the kingdom of God is not a matter of eating and drinking, but of righteousness, peace and joy in the Holy Spirit (Romans 14:17).

> For he has rescued us from the dominion of
> darkness and brought us into the kingdom of
> the Son he loves, in whom we have redemption,
> the forgiveness of sins (Colossians 1:13-14).

But it is equally clear that there is another aspect to the kingdom of God. It is also tomorrow, a future reality.

> This, then, is how you should pray. Our Father
> in heaven, hallowed be your name, your king-
> dom come, you will be done, on earth as it is in
> heaven (Matthew 6:9-10).

> I say to you that many will come from the
> east and the west, and will take their places at
> the feast with Abraham, Isaac and Jacob in the
> kingdom of heaven (Matthew 8:11).

> Those who went ahead and those who fol-
> lowed shouted, "Hosanna!" "Blessed is he who
> comes in the name of the Lord!" "Blessed is the
> coming kingdom of our father David!" (Mark
> 11:9-10).

> I declare to you, brothers, that flesh and
> blood cannot inherit the kingdom of God, not
> does the perishable inherit the imperishable (1
> Corinthians 15:50).

> When the Son of Man comes in his glory,
> and all the angels with him, he will sit on his
> throne in heavenly glory. All the nations will be

gathered before him, and he will separate the sheep from the goats. He will put the sheep on his right and the goats on his left. Then the King will say to those on his right, 'Come, you who are blessed by my Father; take your inheritance, the kingdom prepared for you since the creation of the world (Matthew 25:31-34).

The biblical evidence is compelling. The kingdom of God is both today and tomorrow, present and future, both now and not yet.

OUR INTERPRETATION OF THE KINGDOM

Words have a way of acquiring new meanings. You don't need to be all that old to remember when "rock" had nothing to do with music, or when "grass" referred only to green ground-cover on which you could play golf.

Our dominant instinct is to think of a "kingdom" as a particular territory or populace over which a king or queen rules—a realm or domain. The United Kingdom comes to mind. However, to grasp the biblical understanding of "kingdom," we must examine an older meaning of the word.

"The Lord has established his throne in heaven, and his kingdom rules over all" (Psalm 103:19). By the current standard definition, a kingdom can't rule. In the usual sense a kingdom is the region or the people over whom the monarch rules. The key to understanding the kingdom of God, however, is to discover the older, abstract sense of the word.

The clearest passage in the New Testament to illustrate this concept is found in the third gospel:

As they heard these things, he proceeded to tell a parable, because he was near to Jerusalem, and because they supposed that the kingdom of God was to appear immediately. He said therefore, "A nobleman went into a far country to receive a kingdom and then return. Calling ten of his servants, he gave them ten pounds, and said to them, 'Trade with these till I come.' But his citizens hated him and sent an embassy after him, saying, 'We do not want this man to reign over us.' When he returned, having received the kingdom, he commanded these servants, to whom he had given the money, to be called to him, that he might know what they had gained by trading. (Luke 19:11-15, RSV)

This man of noble birth left the people and place over which he would later rule "to receive a kingdom," that is, the authority to rule. Then, "having received the kingdom," the appropriate authority, he returned. So, the kingdom of God, then, in the biblical context is defined by an abstract rather than a concrete word. Think of his kingdom as his reign, not a specific realm. See it as his dominion, not a particular domain.

Just a few years after Jesus gave this parable, in A.D. 40, Herod the Great went to Rome to be given the authority to rule over Palestine, the land we today call Israel. He received the kingdom and returned to exercise his authority to rule. Thus, in one sentence, "the kingdom of God is the sovereign rule of God, manifested in the person and work of Christ, creating a people over whom he reigns, and issuing in a realm or realms in which the power of his reign is realized."[3]

Putting two and two together, it becomes evident that the Church does not create the kingdom of God. Quite the reverse. The kingdom, God's sovereign rule, produces the Church. Further, it is critical to note that while people can enter the kingdom, the Bible never says they can build it.

Evil has run rampant throughout human history, but at his first coming, Jesus inaugurated God's kingdom. At his second coming, the kingdom will be consummated when Jesus puts all His enemies under his feet. Only partially realized now, the kingdom will be fully realized then.

OUR INVOLVEMENT IN THE KINGDOM

If, as we believe, God is exerting his authority in the world today, then it must follow that individuals, institutions, and nations may choose to live under the standards of his kingdom—more or less. It further follows that Christians ought to assist and encourage others to submit to God's rule, for their own eternal good.

Explaining involvement in the kingdom of God does not require complex theological argumentation—just illustration.

AT THE INDIVIDUAL LEVEL

The way into the kingdom may involve great spiritual struggle, but it is always open. The simplest parallel? Deciding to become a citizen of the United States. One seeks and discovers the process, swears allegiance to his new nation, and submits continuously to its Constitution and laws.

I recall Denver Seminary chancellor, Vernon Grounds, movingly recounting an incident from a century ago, when England's King Edward VII went out walking at night with his wife, who then injured her ankle badly. Imagine! No police or secret service to provide security! They struggled to a farmhouse in the darkness and knocked loudly, only to be greeted by a gruff and profane reply. "Who's there?" the farmer demanded. "King Edward." The farmer cursed the more, thinking it a joke, but the pleading continued. Intending to throw the intruder off the porch, he threw open the door, discovering, to his shame and dismay, that it was indeed the royal couple.

In later years, that farmer repeated his story to anyone who would listen. Invariably he concluded, "To think that I almost didn't let the king in." Jesus Christ can seem like an annoying intruder—not only to individuals, but also to nations like the United States, caught up as we are in a culture war.

AT THE INSTITUTIONAL LEVEL

Our family lore centered on my grandfather, who at sixteen years of age, with a third-grade education and the princely sum of $100 in his pocket, journeyed east from Minnesota to make his fortune. In 1878, he served tenement-dwellers from a push-cart in the streets of Brooklyn. As the years scrolled forward, he moved up to a horse-drawn cart, then a store, and at last a supermarket ahead of its time. One bitter winter day in 1910, when the fire hydrants were frozen solid, the departmentalized market burned to the ground.

Undaunted and trusting God, he shifted gears and developed his business into Dugan Brothers, "Bakers for the Home," which would become the second largest house-to-house baking company in the nation.

When the Japanese bombed Pearl Harbor on the "day of infamy" in 1941, I was just a few weeks shy of ten years of age. The war years gave this impressionable boy repeated opportunities to observe that business in action. It was deliberately run according to biblical standards of integrity. Management cared about the employees, and it was the first in the baking industry to grant, voluntarily, a five-day work-week. The profits of the business, not just the executives' salaries, were tithed to God's work.

Early in World War II, word came that certain commodities would be rationed, including that vital bakery ingredient, sugar. My dad told me one day how he and Uncle Dave had reported to the government exactly how much sugar was stored in their warehouses, as the baseline for future quotas. One exception to the declaration requirement was allowed. If the sugar had already been mixed with other ingredients, it need not be reported.

So what did unscrupulous bakers do? "They would go into their warehouse," my dad said, "take a handful of salt, and throw it up over the stacked hundred pound bags of sugar." They rationalized that the government would never know, besides which they could argue that technically the sugar was already "mixed" with another ingredient. But that was deceiving the authorities, and my father, his brothers, and his father would not stand for it. Forgetting their competitors, they would make an honest declaration and trust God to honor their integrity.

By contrast, let me describe the CEO of Defense-Tech, an imaginary defense contractor from the 1980s. Ronald Reagan had come to the presidency determined to rebuild America's military strength. Defense-Tech's board of directors put great pressure on their CEO to land lucrative defense contracts. His firm often deliberately bid lower than their actual estimates decreed, rationalizing that once into multi-year contracts, with their complex research and development, it would be impossible for the

Pentagon to take their business elsewhere when cost overruns were apologetically announced and explained.

The loss of integrity was palpable. The CEO and his top associates crafted gold-plated remunerative packages through huge salaries, favorable stock options, and grand benefits. They saw to it that they had incredible "golden parachutes" in case they were ousted in an unfriendly takeover. Entertainment was lavish with corporate jets, resort condominiums, country clubs, and nearly unlimited expense accounts for wining and dining high government officials charged with procurement. With his wealth and inflated ego making it seem reasonable, the CEO quit going to church even at Christmas and Easter, and his conscience stopped bothering him just a few weeks into his relationship with a mistress. Insider trading seemed to him a proper perk for a man of his stature, and it was amazing how much influence one could buy in the political arena.

Occasionally it seemed necessary to mislead Defense-Tech's stockholders at annual meetings. Ultimately, however, it was the American people who paid the bill for his corporation's excesses. They were cheated of unconscionable amounts of money, directly and indirectly, by the CEO. The national debt, thanks to the much higher than necessary cost of doing business, climbed on toward the stratosphere.

How do these business institutions compare where the kingdom of God is concerned? The bakery business under an actual business executive, my father, purposefully lived buy the standards of God's kingdom, both corporate and personal. The defense firm, under its hypothetical CEO, could not have cared less about the reign of God in the world, whether corporate or personal. Its only concern was the bottom line. One business with all deliberate speed put itself under the umbrella of the kingdom of God, while the other, motivated by greed, never even contemplated praying, "Thy will be done on earth, as it is in heaven."

Educational institutions also can stand near or far from the kingdom. Consider the college of which I am an alumnus, Wheaton College in a suburb west of Chicago. Its motto, "For Christ and His Kingdom" has characterized the school for more than a century. Professors, Christians all, teach courses from the perspective of an evangelical world-and-life view, having signed personal doctrinal statements, and both they and the students put their names on an agreement to limit their behavior and lifestyles, lest they stain the college's reputation. All students are expected to worship God in regular chapel services.

Again by contrast, compare Wheaton with a typical state university, where moral absolutes are scorned in the classroom and in student housing. Students who protest being assigned a homosexual roommate, for example, are rebuked by the university and assigned to sensitivity classes to help them adjust to the new realities. Women may visit men's rooms, staying all night if they wish. Faculty ridicule Christian students with impunity. It would be unthinkable to allow God and the Bible to be taken seriously in class, and required chapel services would bring on a lawsuit.

AT THE NATIONAL LEVEL

A 1986 high school history textbook, *Triumph of the American Nation,* published by Harcourt, Brace, Jovanovich, provides this version of the historic "Mayflower Compact" of November 11, 1620:

> We whose names are underwritten, the loyall
> subjects of our dread soveraigne Lord, King
> James, of Great Britaine, France, and Ireland
> king, Haveing undertaken for the honour of
> our king and contrie, a voyage to plant the first
> colonie in the Northerne parts of Virginia, doe
> by these presents solemnly and mutualy in the
> presence one of another, covenant and combine
> ourselves togeather into a civil body politick...

What rank dishonesty. What pure, purposeful deception.
The revision of America's history by means of falsifying the
record in official textbooks is scandalous and unforgivable.
America's children are being deprived of the truth about our
nation's history, particularly of its spiritual roots. Here is the true
text of the Mayflower Charter. Note what kind of material (in
italics) was omitted in the fraudulent version above.

> *In the name of God, Amen.* We whose names are
> underwritten, the loyall subjects of our dread
> soveraigne Lord, King James, *by the grace of
> God,* of Great Britaine, France, and Ireland
> king, *defender of the faith, etc.,* Haveing under-
> taken for the *gloire of God, and advancements of
> the Christian faith, and* honour of our king and
> countrie, a voyage to plant the first colonie in
> the Northerne parts of Virginia, doe by these
> presents solemnly and mutualy in the presence
> *of God, and* one of another, covenant and com-
> bine ourselves togeather into a civil body poli-
> tick...

More than one generation is woefully ignorant of America's spiritual heritage. Many of our churches, whose ministries should be characterized by telling "the whole truth, and nothing but the truth," have failed to fill in the historical blanks for their children, youth, and adults. A private evening tour of the Capitol building in Washington (often featured in NAE seminars) regularly proves to be an eye-opener for visitors. Evidence is everywhere—in the inscriptions, in the great paintings displayed in the rotunda, in the sculptures of Statuary Hall—of the importance of people of faith, and specifically of Christianity, in the founding of this country.[4]

Speaking at the National Prayer Breakfast in 1990, Billy Graham referred to the massive changes in Eastern Europe in the previous year. "It's as if God's word to Habakkuk came last year," he said. "'Look at the nations and watch—and be utterly amazed. For I am going to do something in your days that you would not believe even if you were told" (Habakkuk 1:5). Indeed, 1989 was the most important year of this half-century, following 1945 when World War II came to an end.

The collapse of the Berlin Wall was the most stupendous event since Joshua took Jericho. The accelerating rate of Communist yielding of power was captured in a sign stuck in the rubble somewhere:

Poland, 10 years.
Hungary, 10 months.
East Germany, 10 weeks.
Czechoslovakia, 10 days.
Rumania, 10 hours.

Incredibly, in July 1991, a Billy Graham School of Evangelism was conducted in Moscow, with the cooperation of Russian officials.

Where do nations stand in relation to the kingdom of God? Wherever they choose to.

Let me explicitly state that the United States of America never was and never will be the kingdom of God. But, our nation was built on a biblical foundation, its morality flowing from Judeo-Christian principles. Presidents have not hesitated to acknowledge their dependence on God. Abraham Lincoln, faced with the terrible war between the states, proclaimed a national Day of Humiliation, Fasting, and Prayer before God. For most of our history, a vital moral consensus has held us together.

The Soviet Union was committed to atheism, with humanistic values, pushing it into a Communist totalitarianism that simply could not work. Marxism was discredited and democracy, rather than socialism, became the hope of multitudes. As inconceivable as it may have been just a few years earlier, the former "evil empire," having expelled God from national life, now wants to invite him and his truth back, through its children. Thousands of American evangelical volunteers are being trained to teach Christian ethics and morality in the public schools in the Confederation of Independent States.

Is it possible that someday America will be pagan while Russia returns to a historic Christian faith? Pushed by secularizing forces toward godlessness and decadence, America is moving away from the kingdom of God. At the same time, in one of the great ironies of history, Russia shows signs of spiritual hunger that are driving it toward that kingdom.

SUMMARIZING JESUS' KINGDOM TEACHING

It could not be more clear. Persons, be they male or female, rich or poor, may come into the kingdom of God. Institutions, be they corporations or colleges, may situate themselves within the kingdom of God. And nations, be they historically Christian or atheist, may choose to position themselves within, near, or far from the kingdom of God.

The reality of this doctrine undergirds, authorizes, and emphasizes that Christian citizens must be involved in civil government. God is pleased when a nation acknowledges him as Creator and Lord, makes "In God We Trust" its national motto, shapes laws to reflect its Judeo-Christian heritage, elects political leaders who prefer kingdom values, and provides religious freedom through its Bill of Rights as the nation's "first liberty," so that his people may worship him according to the dictates of their consciences.

In the last book of the Bible, the conclusion of history and the end of the nations becomes clear. After a seventh angel sounds his trumpet, loud voices join in chorus: "The kingdom of the world has become the kingdom of our Lord and of his Christ, and he will reign for ever and ever." The nations will be forced to bow and acknowledge the reign of God Almighty, and of Jesus Christ, his eternal Son.

That being the case, can anyone imagine that it would displease our Lord if we, his people, actively attempted to bring our nation more fully within the authority of his kingdom? Which is to say, under the Lordship of Christ? Would that not be true at any level, whether a local school board, the United States Senate, or the White House?

The reverse, of course, would undoubtedly displease him. As followers of Jesus Christ we will fail him miserably if we decline to use our religious and political freedoms to lead the United States to the place where his kingdom's values are recovered and his kingdom's morals are revered.

WHAT

THE

CONSTITUTION

PERMITS

ARE PEOPLE OF FAITH RESTRICTED IN POLITICAL ACTIVITY?

P hil Donahue's television show thrives on the controversial—the more outlandish the better. But until the day I found myself a participant on his show in December 1983, I had actually seen little more than occasional glimpses of the program.

Phil's intent for that day was to parlay President Ronald Reagan's November radio and television spots for the Layman's National Bible Week into a national controversy. The president had not simply referred to "the Bible" in his public service announcements, but had urged Americans to read "God's Word." In short, he had dared express publicly his belief about the Bible—his religious conviction. To Donahue and much of his audience, such contentious commercials were out of bounds.

The cast of characters fascinated me. Two panelists were to critique the president: a Southern Baptist minister from North Carolina who also served as a vice president of his state's ACLU chapter, and an atheist from New York who thought it relevant to tell the world he was a homosexual and proud of it. I was expected to support the president, along with Martin Marty, church history professor, author, and a regular contributor to the *Christian Century*. While Marty did support Reagan's right to make the announcements, he obviously wished the president hadn't done so. Marty was generally critical throughout the show. It became three against one, and Donahue wasn't exactly on my side either.

One theme kept recurring in the first half of the show: the president had done something worse than malevolent. He had violated the Constitution of the United States. Finally it came time to interrupt. "Phil, I have a question that needs answering. Several times today I've heard somebody on this panel or in the audience say that the president did something 'unconstitutional' when he made those announcements. It's time somebody explained just how the president transgressed the Constitution he is sworn to uphold. Who will point out the constitutional chapter and verse that he violated?"

Silence. Not wanting the question to go unanswered, I suggested that the only possible text in anybody's mind was the First Amendment, whose first sixteen words I then quoted. But that Amendment mentions Congress, not the president. It mentions a law, not the speech, remarks, or media announcements of the chief executive. The First Amendment authorizes free exercise of religion, a right the president had used.

"If President Reagan has not disobeyed the First Amendment to the Constitution, then what other section are we talking about?" No one said anything. Martin Marty assuredly knew I was right, and I suspect Donahue did, too. But the discussion was abruptly turned to other things, without an answer from anyone.

Pity those who, over the years, have "learned" most of what they know about constitutional law (or morality, ethics, and religion for that matter) from lightweight shows such as Donahue's. Ignorance abounds around the nation, especially where the Constitution is concerned.

A Hearst national survey marking the Constitution's 1987 bicentennial, found that nearly 50 percent of Americans thought the Constitution contained Karl Marx's axiom, "From each according to his ability, to each according to his need." Six out of ten thought that the president, acting alone, could appoint or fire a Supreme Court justice. The same number were unaware that the Bill of Rights is the first ten amendments to the Constitution.

MISREADING THE CONSTITUTION

Profound misunderstanding of the Constitution has deeply affected evangelical Christians. Unfortunately, many evangelicals have hidden their faith, meekly but unnecessarily submitting to the media elite's insistence that religiously based convictions should have no part in public policy—that we must have what Richard John Neuhaus calls "The Naked Public Square." In some cases, they have even acquiesced in the matter of elections, having been cajoled into thinking that the personal moral qualifications and convictions of candidates are not proper political considerations.

Evangelicals have been rhetorically beaten about the head and shoulders until they are black and blue with one of the most misunderstood phrases of our time: "separation of church and state." Because they assume such separation to be constitutional, they knuckle under. But if we are to fulfill the biblical mandate to "render unto Caesar what is Caesar's" then since the Constitution of the United States of America is our Caesar, we must know…what is constitutional?

The "Grand Experiment" that became the United States of America has the Declaration of Independence for its foundation and the Constitution for its political structure. Several years ago Warren Burger, chief justice of the Supreme Court, sent a message to a National Day of Prayer banquet. His nephew Steve, an evangelical leader from Seattle, was his courier. The chief justice had discovered this marvelous quotation in the writings of James Madison and wanted to share it: "We would not have a Constitution, were it not for the intervention of God."

That Constitution—the result of much compromise—was not perfect, but it has served magnificently. Over a century ago, British prime minister William Gladstone (who, from his side of the Atlantic, might have been expected to be critical of our breakaway nation) lauded our national charter: "I have always regarded that Constitution as the most remarkable work known to me in modern times to have been produced by the human intellect, at a single stroke (so to speak), in its application to political affairs."[1]

About two-thirds of the world's constitutions have been adopted or revised since 1970, and only fourteen predate World War II.[2] Ours is the oldest written national constitution still in force in the world today, the source of the United States' remarkable political stability. When Sen. Daniel Patrick Moynihan (D-NY) was ambassador to the United Nations, he discovered that only seven nations going as far back as 1914 had not suffered a change of government through violent revolution.

The Constitution was signed on September 17, 1787, and technically ratified by the ninth state, New Hampshire, on June 21 of the following year. It seemed best to await the action of New York and Virginia, however, since the government could not succeed without them. After they ratified, the Continental

Congress put the Constitution into effect on September 13, 1788.

The framers stated their intentions in a magnificent preamble:

> We the People of the United States, in Order to form a more perfect Union, establish Justice, insure domestic Tranquility, provide for the common defense, promote the general Welfare, and secure the Blessings of Liberty to ourselves and our Posterity, do ordain and establish this Constitution for the United States of America.

Their foremost purpose was to establish a nation that would be ruled by law, not by men. The Constitution itself is basically a secular document which mentions religion only twice, the first time in the final paragraph of Article VI:

> The Senators and Representatives before mentioned, and the Members of the several State Legislatures, and all executive and judicial Officers, both of the United States and of the several States, shall be bound by Oath or Affirmation, to support this Constitution; but no religious Test shall ever be required as a Qualification to any Office of public Trust under the United States.

NO RELIGIOUS TEST

The framers made provision for those unwilling to take an oath of office, usually implying formal calling upon God to bear witness to one's sincerity, by allowing officeholders merely to affirm their commitment to support the Constitution. The words following could not be more clear. They have always been observed in the legal and technical sense that no religious belief has ever been listed as a requirement to hold any federal political office.

On the other hand, the voting public may sometimes apply an unwritten religious test. Imagine a school board election in a Bible-belt state, with a Southern Baptist running against an avowed atheist. It would be a rainy day in the Sahara before the nonbeliever would win. Imagine a last-minute revelation that one of two candidates in a congressional race is a "Moonie." No doubt about the outcome there. But one is not limited to hypothesizing about religious tests applied by voters.

In 1928, Alfred E. Smith had no chance for the presidency against Herbert Hoover because of anti-Catholic sentiment. In 1960, the anti-Catholic vote was still a reality, but it did not prevent John F. Kennedy from winning the presidency. A Williamsburg Charter survey in February 1988 found that only 8 percent would today refuse to vote for a Catholic, but 13 percent would never vote for "a born-again Baptist" for president, and 21 percent were unwilling to vote for a candidate who had been a minister of a church. On the other side, 62 percent were unwilling to vote for an atheist for president.

Given the growing secularism in America, increasing numbers of voters consciously or unconsciously may discriminate against candidates with strong religious beliefs. The summer of 1994 saw a flurry of attacks against conservative Christian political activity, including "fire-breathing Christian radical right" rhetoric by a member of Congress. The Anti-Defamation League of B'nai B'rith published a report entitled *The Religious Right: The Assault on Tolerance & Pluralism in America.*

As for that report, seventy-five Jewish leaders purchased a quarter-page advertisement in the *New York Times*, headlined: "Should Jews Fear the 'Christian Right'?" They answered their own question: "We...reject the implications of this report and deplore its publication." Citing "discreditable techniques [such] as insinuation and guilt by association," they harshly rebuke the ADL: "It ill behooves an organization dedicated to fighting against defamation to engage in defamation of its own."

Some concerns about religious candidates, however, may be valid. In the summer of 1986, Norman Lear's People for the American Way (PAW) ballyhooed an "election project" targeted at religious intolerance in political campaigns. It was obvious that PAW believed there was plenty of it, especially among Christian candidates.

PAW insisted on five standards. Candidates should not claim to be better qualified because of religious affiliation; assert that God endorses their views; question their opponents' religious faith or personal morality on the basis of their political stands; claim that God endorses their aspirations for public office; or accept support that violates these guidelines.

Who could disagree? Frankly, I've not seen many of these "violations" among evangelical candidates. Interestingly, when I ran for Congress in 1976, I somehow instinctively knew how an evangelical should behave. In spite of the fact that Lear's organization had not yet been conceived and these restrictions revealed, I complied with every one of PAW's guidelines. The offensive Christian candidates PAW was describing were most likely to be found in made-for-television productions.

What irony. PAW is oblivious to the beam in its own eye. It regularly set up negative religious tests, labeled committed Christians "ultra-fundamentalists," called President Reagan "evangelist-in-chief," and ridiculed anyone who believed a phi-losophy of secular humanism existed. Worse yet, PAW conduct-ed a national media campaign that precluded the appointment of an outstanding evangelical to the Justice Department, largely on the basis of his personal faith. That's not "The American Way"—the constitutional way.

The second place religion is mentioned in the Constitution is in a portion added four years later. The chief barrier to ratifica-tion had been criticism that the Constitution lacked a Bill of Rights to prevent tyranny by the majority.

While the Constitution was being drafted in Philadelphia, Thomas Jefferson was serving as Minister to France. In December, on studying the document, he wrote to James Madison: "I will now tell you what I do not like. First, the omis-sion of a bill of rights, providing clearly, and without the aid of sophism, for freedom of religion, freedom of the press, protec-tion against standing armies, restriction of monopolies…"[3]

On July 31, 1788, Jefferson again wrote to Madison from Paris, revealing his intention for such a package: "I hope…a bill of rights will be formed to guard the people against the federal government, as they are already guarded against their State gov-ernments in most instances."

It is worth noting that Jefferson's letter did not express con-cern about protecting the government from religious influence, but precisely the opposite—protecting religion, as practiced by the people, from the government. One of the purposes of sepa-rating church and state was to limit the state. If the state is not limited, the church must vacate any area the state decides to claim for itself.

James Madison's assurances that the first Congress would pass a Bill of Rights calmed the fears of many. The promise was kept when Congress adopted ten amendments in September 1789, and their ratification by the states was completed on December 15, 1791.

THE FIRST AMENDMENT

America was the first country ever to establish religious freedom as its "first liberty." In the words of the first two clauses of the First Amendment are the guarantees of this precious freedom:

> Congress shall make no law respecting an establishment of religion, or prohibiting the free exercise thereof; or abridging the freedom of speech, or of the press; or the right of the people peaceably to assemble, and to petition the Government for a redress of grievances.

• **The no establishment clause,** "Congress shall make no law respecting an establishment of religion..." means primarily that the federal government must not give preference to any one religion. No church, to put it another way, could be elevated to an exclusive position of favor and power. The clause makes all the sense in the world when we recall how many newcomers to America, like the Pilgrims, were fleeing religious persecution by established churches in Europe.

Still, at the time of the Revolution, nine of the thirteen colonies had established churches, six being Anglican and three Congregational. Paradoxically, many who fled religious persecution became intolerant of dissenters in their own states. By 1787, however, four of those churches had been disestablished.[4] The Framers clearly intended that there would be no establishment of a national church. Later, by the "doctrine of incorporation," the fourteenth Amendment would apply the no establishment clause to the several states.

• **The free exercise clause,** "Congress shall make no law...prohibiting the free exercise thereof," means that citizens of all faiths or of no faith would have liberty not only to hold their deepest religious beliefs—something that cannot be prevented even in a totalitarian society—but also to express and practice them.

There are limitations, however. While the freedom to believe is absolute, the freedom to act cannot be. If a religion required human sacrifice, for instance, society would have the obligation to interfere with the free exercise of that religion in order to protect the lives of potential victims.

SEPARATION OF CHURCH AND STATE

It surprises many people to discover that the concept of separation of church and state is not found in the Constitution, but I don't make much of that. The word *trinity* is not found in the Bible either, but it is the ideal word to express a historic, orthodox doctrine of the Bible. Not incidentally, the concept of separation of church and state was for decades enunciated in the Soviet constitution.

Evangelicals believe strongly in the separation of church and state, as historically understood by the Founding Fathers. Both institutions originate with God, and each has its proper spheres of responsibility. For example, the obligation to evangelize belongs to the church; the duty to govern belongs to the state.

Theologian R. C. Sproul cites St. Augustine as teaching that "government is not a necessary evil; rather, it is necessary because of evil." As a matter of fact, the Bible spells out three functions for the state: to provide order, to promote well-doing, and to punish wrongdoing.[5]

To see how the spheres of responsibility work out, take the matter of discipline. Should the church interfere with the government's criminal justice system by springing from prison someone it presumes to be innocent, or by lynching someone the church feels mistakenly to have been acquitted of murder? Either would be preposterous. On the other hand, should government interfere with a church's internal discipline by forcing it against its will to hire a certain person, or by overruling its excommunication of an openly sinning member who is having a publicly known affair? Either of these would be absurd too.

Tragically, the preposterous sometimes happens. In 1984, after a week-long trial, a Tulsa jury awarded $390,000 in actual and punitive damages to a woman disfellowshiped by the Collinsville, Oklahoma, Church of Christ, for having an affair with a politician. If there was ever a clear violation of the historic concept of separation of church and state, this is it.

What the Framers intended constitutional church/state separation to mean is quite different from the Supreme Court's interpretation since 1947.[6] In that period much greater emphasis was placed on the no establishment clause, with free exercise apparently receding into secondary consideration. It seems as if the High Court was constitutionally allergic to anything in public life tasting of religion. Decision after decision seemed designed to segregate education and legislation from religiously based values. It is almost as if the Court's ultimate goal was to create a fully secularized state. The judicial branch of government was subtly shifting the United States from separation of church and state to separation of religion and state.

In the *Lemon v. Kurtzman* case in 1971, then Chief Justice Burger set forth three tests that would be used to decide establishment cases in the future: "First, the statute must have a secular legislative purpose; second, its principal or primary effect must be one that neither advances nor inhibits religion; finally, the statute must not foster 'an excessive government entanglement with religion.'"[7]

Current Chief Justice William Rehnquist has severely criticized this judge-made law. Because the three-pronged Lemon test is based on a "historically false doctrine," the approach is inadequate for deciding establishment clause cases. And what is the faulty doctrine? In his learned dissent in the *Jaffre* silent prayer case, Rehnquist asserted that the court, ever since 1947, has been interpreting the First Amendment's ban on "establishing" religion erroneously. "The 'wall of separation between church and state' is a metaphor based on bad history, a metaphor which has proved useless as a guide to judging," he said. "It should be frankly and explicitly abandoned."[8]

Arguing that "the true meaning of the establishment clause can only be seen in its history," Rehnquist wrote that the clause "did not require government neutrality between religion and irreligion, nor did it prohibit the federal government from providing non-discriminatory aid to religion. There is simply no historical foundation for the proposition that the framers intended to build the 'wall of separation.'" The wall, he said, in recent opinions has become a "blurred, indistinct, and variable barrier." As NAE's counsel puts it, "The *Lemon* test is a lemon."

Absolute separation never has been constitutionally necessary, and always has been impossible in a practical sense. Given an absolute separation of church and state, the local fire department would not respond to the alarm—and should not—if your church building were ablaze. There would be no need to seek town planning commission approval for expanding church facilities. Why not get maximum square footage by building over the sidewalks to the very street itself? Government, under absolute separation, would have no right to insist on parking lots, size limitations, or anything else. If there were absolute separation of church and state, the crier would not open daily sessions at a beautiful marble building on Capitol Hill as he now impressively does: "Oyez, Oyez, Oyez! All persons having business before the Honorable, the Supreme Court of the United States, are admonished to draw near and give their attention, for the Court is now sitting. God save the United States and this Honorable Court."

THE WILLIAMSBURG CHARTER

Given the controversies over religion in public life, The Williamsburg Charter Project of 1987-88 was a godsend. It was a blue-ribbon national project designed to celebrate the genius of the First Amendment's religious liberty provisions and to attempt to construct a new national consensus on the meaning of that amendment. It was hoped that the nation would then be able to reaffirm and rededicate itself to that understanding.

Led by sociologist and author Os Guinness, this project became an officially recognized program of the Commission on the bicentennial of the United States Constitution. The Williamsburg Charter[9] document itself is a superb achievement, drafted by a divergent group of scholars and publicly signed in Williamsburg, Virginia, on June 25, 1988. The nearly two hundred signers were invited not as "celebrity" public figures, but as leaders pledging themselves to uphold and defend the charter's principles.

Judging by the diversity of signers, an incredible new consensus was achieved. Representing government were Chief Justices William H. Rehnquist and Warren E. Burger; former Presidents Jimmy Carter and Gerald Ford; and the democratic speaker and the minority leader of the House, Reps. Jim Wright and Robert Michel. Representing political parties were the chairmen of the Republican and Democratic National Committees. Representing the Bicentennial Commission were, among others, ideological opposites Sen. Edward M. Kennedy (D-MA) and Mrs. Phyllis Schlafly.

Representing American communities of faith were Catholic, Jewish, and other religious leaders, along with the presidents of the National Association of Evangelicals and the National Council of Churches. Representing education and public policy were the top leaders of the National Education Association and the conservative Heritage Foundation. Representing minorities and ethnic groups were Coretta Scott King, Beverly LaHaye, and others. There were signers from business, labor, and law.

Most revealing was the diversity of those who signed on behalf of organizations specifically concerned with religion and public life. Juxtaposed against evangelical leaders such as Charles W. Colson of Prison Fellowship, James Dobson of Focus on the Family, and Samuel Ericsson of the Christian Legal Society were Arie Brouwer of the National Council of Churches, John Buchanan and Norman Lear of People for the American Way, and Robert Maddox of Americans United for Separation of Church and State.

I was one of eight signers privileged to make public comments during the Williamsburg ceremony, because the earliest faith characterizing American life was evangelical Christianity. But for me personally, it was a moving moment. The ceremony took place in front of the restored capitol building in Colonial Williamsburg, where John Robinson, my forebear, had served as the first Speaker in Virginia's House of Burgesses, in turn the first representative government in America.

Such a diverse group normally would never have put their signatures on one document about religion in public life—unless it were an unparalleled accomplishment. It is. It articulates a proper balance. While differences of opinion still exist, these opinion leaders arrived at a new consensus of principles, the vanguard of a new civility in public debate.

To echo the famous E. F. Hutton television commercial, when The Williamsburg Charter speaks, people listen. Here are some highlights from the twenty-three page charter:

> The First Amendment Religious Liberty provisions provide the United States' most distinctive answer to one of the world's most pressing questions in the late-twentieth century. They address the problem: How do we live with each other's deepest differences?

> ...the need for...today can best be addressed by remembering that the two clauses are essentially one provision for preserving religious liberty. Both parts, no establishment and free exercise, are to be comprehensively understood as being in the service of religious liberty as a positive good. At the heart of the establishment clause is the prohibition of state sponsorship of religion and at the heart of the free exercise clause is the prohibition of state interference with religious liberty.

The result is neither a naked public square where all religion is excluded, nor a sacred public square with any religion established or semi-established. The result, rather, is a civil public square in which citizens of all religious faiths, or none, engage one another in the continuing democratic discourse.[10]

RELIGIOUS INFLUENCE ON GOVERNMENT

Evangelical Christians, and all people with strong religious convictions, should take heart. Nothing in the Constitution implies that it is improper for religion to have an influence on the government—not Article VI, not the First Amendment, not a derived but unwritten concept of separation of church and state. Only a distorted interpretation of the First Amendment, making it "an intellectual pretzel" (to use George Will's metaphor), can be used to intimidate religious citizens from becoming political activists.

Once again, the Williamsburg Charter consensus is crystal clear when it refers to the "right to influence":

Too often in recent disputes over religion and public affairs, some have insisted that any evidence of religious influence on public policy represents an establishment of religion and is therefore precluded as an improper "imposition." Such exclusion of religion from public life is historically unwarranted, philosophically inconsistent, and profoundly undemocratic. The Framers' intention is indisputably ignored when public policy debates can appeal to the theses of Adam Smith and Karl Marx, or Charles Darwin and Sigmund Freud, but not to the Western religious tradition in general and the Hebrew and Christian Scriptures in particular. Many of the most dynamic social movements in American history, including that of civil rights, were legitimately inspired and shaped by religious motivation.

Freedom of conscience and the right to influence public policy on the basis of religiously informed ideas are inseparably linked. In short, a key to democratic renewal is the fullest possible participation in the most open possible debate.

To double your appreciation of the conclusions just read the Charter and remind yourself again of the highly respected, bipartisan group of signers. They stand behind the rights of people like us, whose beliefs are shaped by Scripture.

Unfortunately, the Internal Revenue Code puts some limitations on how much of their resources churches and other 501(c)(3) organizations may use in seeking to influence government on issues. Further, the code declares illegal direct participation in political campaigns, either for or against any candidate for public office. It is critical to note that only *institutional* campaign involvement by churches is out of order; the individual involvement of church members is a right guaranteed by the Constitution itself.

In giving to all citizens the right to influence their government, the Constitution nowhere denies those rights to citizens who hold deep religious convictions. Evangelicals have all the room they need to be involved in politics and government.

Those who attempt to browbeat evangelicals into political silence are, at best, intellectually inconsistent. At worst, they are deliberately dishonest.

When Geraldine Ferraro was selected as Walter Mondale's vice presidential running mate in the 1984 campaign, religion became a major issue. Although a Catholic, Ferraro fell back on the old saw about being personally opposed to abortion, but not wanting to impose her religious views on others. When Archbishop (now Cardinal) John O'Connor pressed Ferraro, New York Governor Mario Cuomo defended her, arguing that abortion is a religious issue which should have no place in the campaign.

In a speech at the Notre Dame Law School in September 1984, Rep. Henry Hyde (R-IL) gave an illustration of today's unacceptable double standard concerning religious input in politics. He read from a letter written to the president of the National Conference of Catholic Bishops which appeared in the New York Diocesan newspaper, *Catholic New York*, on July 7, 1983:

> As an American and a Catholic I am proud of you. It would have been easy to compromise your position so as to offend no one. You chose instead to tend to your duties as shepherds, to teach the moral law as best you can. You can do no more. Our Church has sometimes been accused of not having spoken out when it might have. Now you, our Bishops, show the courage and moral judgment to meet this issue

of nuclear holocaust with a collective expression
of where the Church in America stands.[11]

Hyde then stated simply: "This letter was signed by the
present governor of New York, Mario Cuomo." Touché.
Apparently for Cuomo, when it comes to nuclear freezes, religious persuasion is good. But when it comes to abortion, religious influence is bad.

Evangelicals had better not let themselves be bullied by political opponents brandishing separation of church and state arguments. Most of their adversaries would be cheering them on if
their religious convictions put them on the other side of certain
issues.

Just as the Apostle Paul exercised his rights as a Roman citizen,[12] we need to understand our constitutional rights—and
exercise them. And we must let no mythical "wall" stand in our
way.

WHAT NOTABLE VICTORIES HAVE ALREADY BEEN WON?

I n its infinite wisdom, the Internal Revenue Service in 1978 provoked a reaction that led to unprecedented evangelical political involvement in the 1980s. The IRS proposed a number of regulations for private schools which presumed them to be racist—and no longer qualified for tax-exempt status if their student bodies did not contain an "adequate" percentage of minority students, based on their local communities. Had the scheme gone through, schools innocent of the accusation "white flight academies" would probably have been forced to close their doors.

The regulations comprised nothing less than an unjust threat to put a large segment of the Christian school movement out of business. When the IRS scheduled December dates for public comments, during my second month in Washington, I testified. The IRS had to be stopped, lest faceless bureaucrats label hundreds of Christian schools as segregationist. They would be presumed guilty, based on mere numbers, until they could somehow prove themselves innocent. That's not the way American justice is supposed to work.

The proposed regulations sparked a storm of protest. One testimony about a Hebrew school located in a 50 percent Hispanic Miami neighborhood blew the IRS's assumptions to smithereens. How could the IRS suspect that school of discriminating against Hispanics, most of whom were Roman Catholic? Few of them were likely to seek admission to a Jewish school. Should the IRS force Jews to recruit Hispanics, thus making the federal government indirectly responsible for Jewish evangelization of them? Try fitting that into the First Amendment.

The impact of the collective testimony, backed by a mass of protest from Christians across the country, was overwhelming. The IRS postponed implementation of its proposals and, in 1980, Congress passed the Ashbrook-Dornan amendments that prohibited the IRS from yanking tax-exempt status from religious schools. If the IRS had not seen the light, at least it had felt the heat. But that's often how things work in politics.

Key to the victory were the grass roots objections of thousands of Christian citizens. To produce future pressure on the IRS, Congress, or the White House, it was obvious that evangelicals needed reliable information about issues affecting them in Washington. That's why the newsletter *NEA Washington Insight*[1] was first published in March 1979. For sixteen years now our monthly newsletter has been providing inside information and interpreting what government is doing or threatening to do.

THE BIRTH OF THE
PRO-FAMILY MOVEMENT

It was the midpoint of the Carter administration when I came to Washington. I discovered that most of the religious community in the capital felt it was more difficult to establish contact in the Carter White House than with any administration since

Eisenhower's. I theorized that the president's staff wanted to de-emphasize Carter's widely publicized "born-again" faith. The fewer religious leaders around him, the less people would be reminded of his faith, already too prominent for certain staffers' liking.

In any case, things began to change in the summer of 1979, after Carter brought Southern Baptist minister Robert Maddox to his White House staff as a speechwriter and then assigned him liaison duties to the religious community. All his skills would be needed for a major conflict brewing during Carter's final year. A special White House program was about to galvanize Christians and others into the pro-family movement.

When we first got wind of the White House Conference on the Family, that was its name. But by 1980 it had been renamed the White House Conference on Families. By this subtle shift, liberal social scientists could avoid the implication that there was a traditionally definable entity known as "the family"—persons related by blood, marriage, or adoption. That, of course, is the biblical definition. Conference planners wanted to install the American Home Economics Society's definition: "People who share the same living or cooking quarters and have a long-term commitment to each other." The sky would have been the limit on such "family" groupings.

Evangelicals were troubled, but then encouraged when some of their leaders secured presidential appointments to the confer-ence. While pro-family forces did succeed at many points, a composite of positions adopted at those meetings formed a liberal social agenda—in many ways anti-family. To implement them would have required heavy federal funding. Fortunately, the issue became moot when Jimmy Carter was defeated for reelection. With Ronald Reagan as president the liberals' agenda was blocked.

A few weeks before the end of President Carter's term, my wife and I found ourselves the only religious leaders at a White House reception with President and Mrs. Carter. A senior staffer confided that the president wanted us there because, while our differences on many issues were known to him, among evangelical groups NAE had treated him fairly and courteously.

By God's providence and the president's thoughtfulness we were at that reception. But far too many Christians exhibit anger and even hatred toward political opponents and by so doing remove themselves from the political process. But most importantly, Jesus' command to "love your enemies" has not been cancelled.

BORN-AGAIN CANDIDATES

There was one political mistake evangelical voters would not be able to repeat in the 1980 presidential election. In the past they might have voted for a presidential candidate solely on the basis of a common Christian faith. Not this time. Incumbent President Jimmy Carter, Republican challenger Ronald Reagan, and independent John B. Anderson all identified themselves as evangelicals. Each one seemed to have a credible profession of faith.

Back in 1976, Jimmy Carter's unabashed acknowledgment of his born-again Christian faith escaped no one's notice. It may have helped him capture the Democratic presidential nomination. It also brought evangelical Christianity into the limelight, especially through Newsweek's "Year of the Evangelical" cover article. UPI reporter Wesley Pippert analyzed Carter as making a unique attempt to be a servant-leader to the nation. He was a strong family man and dedicated to peace.

Notwithstanding his advantage as incumbent and four years' experience in the world's toughest job, in 1980 Carter was not running strong. His economic and energy track record was poor, and his foreign policy skills were mocked by the Iranian hostage situation. Evangelicals were puzzled and disillusioned. Did they not have a right to expect that a fellow-believer would share their views on abortion and school prayer? His explanation that his sincerely held view of separation of church and state did not allow his spiritual convictions to shape his political positions would not wash. Further, why had he failed to include evangelicals in top-level positions in his administration?

Republican nominee Ronald Reagan was running on his track record as governor of California. He had created a surplus from the state's deficit and eliminated a great deal of welfare fraud. Almost instinctively he identified with many of the moral and spiritual concerns of evangelicals, such as the sanctity of human life, the importance of returning voluntary prayer to the nation's schools, and the value of biblical morality. He convinced evangelicals that he would include qualified persons from their ranks in his administration. Reagan's personal faith was not as clearly expressed as Carter's and Anderson's, but if untutored, it did appear genuine.

Moderately liberal congressman John Anderson entered the competition for the Republican nomination in June but, failing that, became an independent candidate. Anderson's 1964 designation as the National Association of Evangelicals' "Layman of the Year" was included in his official biography, but he would never have been granted that recognition in 1980. A gifted leader, his peers had voted him the second most persuasive orator in the House. He admirably used his rhetorical skills to swing the crucial votes that passed fair housing legislation in 1968.

Carter's campaign practically indicted Anderson with introducing a constitutional amendment to make Christianity the official faith of the nation in 1961, 1963, and again in 1965. Anderson now repudiated that action as immature. Many of his social views had moved so far to the left that evangelicals were dumbfounded. It seemed incredible that Anderson cosponsored gay rights legislation and supported unrestricted abortion rights, to the embarrassment of his evangelical denomination.[2]

THE NEW RELIGIOUS RIGHT

Evangelicals were forced to make a thoughtful choice in this election. Not only did the dramatically divergent positions of Carter, Reagan, and Anderson demand careful evaluation, but a formidable new entity made its debut in presidential politics in 1980.

The astute strategists who brought the new religious right into existence saw evangelicals as a huge block of generally unmotivated voters. Surveys showed that these religious folk were more conservative than the general population in matters of economics and national defense. How could they be activated to add votes that would put conservatives in the win column? It dawned on new right strategists that issues like abortion, prayer in schools, and pornography would be of great moral concern to Bible-believing Christians, once they were informed. They went after the evangelical vote.

Meanwhile, the Republican Party had been cultivating evangelical leaders. I was part of a small cadre of leaders who had been getting acquainted with potential Republican presidential nominees—and, eventually with the Democratic nominee, President Jimmy Carter. In August 1979 we met with former Texas governor John Connally on his Texas ranch. Then followed fall meetings with Ronald Reagan, Sen. Howard Baker (R-

TN), and Rep. Phil Crane (R-IL). In early spring we met George Bush in Chicago.

During the 1980 National Religious Broadcasters convention, twelve of us were invited to the White House for breakfast with Jimmy Carter. The president remained for forty minutes of frank discussion—better than the fifteen pledged by his staff.

As promised, Republicans did indeed pitch their platform to evangelicals. They endorsed efforts to restore voluntary prayer to public schools, supported a constitutional amendment banning abortion on demand, and favored tuition-tax credits that would allow parents a realistic possibility of educating their children in Christian schools. In a highly controversial section, they even pledged to nominate federal judges who opposed abortion. Democrats, on the other hand, took opposing positions, even endorsing the drive for homosexual rights and against discrimination on the basis of sexual orientation. It was clear that many evangelical concerns were of little interest to Democrats.

As everyone knows, by the time Ronald Reagan arrived at the Republican convention in Detroit, the only suspense was his choice of a running mate. President Carter easily outdistanced Sen. Ted Kennedy (D-MA) for renomination. The election in November promised to be a cliffhanger.

But it wasn't, and evangelicals were a major part of the reason. The nation's political crust shifted massively in 1980. The American public heeded the Republican slogan to vote "for a change," and commentators were comparing Reagan's victory to the dramatic turnabout election of Franklin D. Roosevelt in 1932. Indeed, until then in this century only Alf Landon in 1936 and George McGovern in 1972, among major party candidates, won fewer electoral college votes than did Jimmy Carter in his 489-49 loss. He became only the eighth incumbent to lose a presidential reelection bid.

Millions deserted Carter at the polls, all the while probably regarding him as a decent man, personally honest, and with good intentions. Many of those were the so-called born-again voters who, ironically, probably had been responsible for putting him into the White House in 1976. While it is difficult to find trustworthy figures on the born-again vote in 1968 or 1972, one estimate is that somewhere between 5 and 7.5 million evangelicals switched *to* Carter in 1976.[3]

Disappointed, disillusioned, distanced, or whatever, evangelicals who had once strongly supported Carter switched allegiance. According to the ABC News-Lou Harris survey, the white, Baptist vote in the South revealed what happened. In 1976, that vote had preferred Carter to Gerald Ford 56 percent to 43 percent. By 1980, white Southern Baptists preferred Reagan over their own Southern Baptist Sunday school teaching Jimmy Carter by 56 percent to 34 percent.[4] Reading Bob Maddox's book *Preacher in the White House,* I got the feeling that neither he nor Jimmy Carter ever really understood why evangelicals forsook the president. Perhaps it is more accurate to suggest that they never accepted him.[5]

Evangelical leaders did not set out to construct an evangelical voting bloc, although some of the new religious right leaders did. When the election's smoke had cleared, however, the Moral Majority's Jerry Falwell and others minimized the impact of the evangelical vote. The humble stance was strategic. While grander claims might have been justified, they would have overly alarmed their opponents.

What was the actual evangelical impact upon the election of Ronald Reagan? An analogy from baseball will help to explain. If a team wins an 8-7 game, any player on the winning team who scored or batted in a run could technically claim that "his" run furnished the victory margin. On the other hand, that run or RBI would have been ineffective without the other runs.

In the election of Ronald Reagan, analysts acknowledged that a bloc of born-again voters at least batted in a run.

DISAPPOINTMENT WITH REAGAN

One thing about Reagan disappointed evangelicals. He and Nancy, citing security problems, failed to attend worship services on Sundays. Instead, on weekends they either remained in the White House, helicoptered to Camp David, or flew to their ranch above Santa Barbara. That makes Nancy Reagan's comments about spiritual things, never mentioned publicly before their last summer in office, fascinating. The First Lady addressed a national conference of Youth for Christ in the nation's capital on July 27, 1988:

> My father, who died six years ago, was a brilliant man, an internationally known brain surgeon. He was a person of tremendous self-confidence and intellect. So it is ironic that his spiritual life was influenced by a small, petty event that happened in his childhood. When he was a boy, there was a contest in his Sunday school class. The winner was to receive a Bible. My father knew he'd won the contest, for even then he was totally confident in himself and his abilities. He simply couldn't accept it when the Bible was given to the child of the minister. And in reaction, my father, feeling wronged

and disillusioned, allowed no place for faith in his life for the next eighty years.

He would take my mother and me to church and Sunday school, but he'd leave and come back only when it was time to pick us up. My mother had a very deep religious faith; she read her Bible every night. And it was that deep and abiding faith that helped her tremendously at the end of her life.

But my father didn't have that and at the end of his life, he was terribly frightened. He was even afraid to go to sleep for fear he wouldn't wake up. He'd move from chair to chair trying to keep awake and, I guess, alive. I can't tell you how much it hurt to see him this way—this man who had always been so supremely confident and strong in my eyes. My husband wrote him two long letters explaining the encompassing comfort he'd receive if he'd just put himself in the Lord's hands.

I was at the hospital with him, but my father never mentioned to me what happened next; the doctors told me. Two days before he died, he asked to see the hospital chaplain. I don't know what the chaplain did or what he said, but whatever it was, it was the right thing and it gave my father comfort. I noticed he was calmer and not as frightened. When he died

the next day, he was at peace, finally. And I was
so happy for him. My prayers were answered.[6]

Nancy Reagan's father paid a tragic, lifelong price for a
momentary loss of integrity in the church. When we evangelicals
seek to bring about change, when we relate to government,
media, and even our own constituency, God forbid that we ever
do so without absolute integrity.

But for the sovereignty of God, America would not have had
much of an opportunity to evaluate the presidency of Ronald
Reagan. Do you remember the intrepid humor of the president,
when he scanned the doctors surrounding his hospital gurney,
prepared to remove the would-be assassin's bullet? "I hope you're
all Republicans!" Chief of the surgical team that day at George
Washington University Hospital was Dr. Benjamin Aaron, who
later suggested in personal conversation with me that "there was
some kind of divine providence riding with that bullet."

MORAL ISSUES

Despite Reagan's early triumphs, evangelicals were restless. Their
social concerns had been left on the back burner for long months
while the president and Congress tackled the economy. During
Reagan's first term, NAE and other religious groups battled for a
constitutional amendment to allow prayer in schools, a human
life amendment to protect the unborn, tuition tax-credit legislation, and against the appointment of an ambassador to the
Vatican. Although the votes were not there in Congress, the
White House was open to us—in sharp contrast to the previous
administration.

For nearly a year, the White House laid plans for a religious
leaders' luncheon with the president. I worked with the White

House to adopt criteria for the invitations and then to assemble the guest list. As a matter of course Catholic, Jewish, and Protestant leaders were invited, but this time evangelicals were represented at more than token levels. On April 13, 1982, the president hosted more than one hundred national religious leaders, many of whom, like NAE denominational heads and parachurch leaders, were eating in the State Dining Room for the first time. More than half of those invited were evangelicals.

Ronald Reagan, moreover, was willing to go out of his way to address evangelicals. While Presidents Ford in 1976 and Reagan in 1981 had addressed combined NAE and National Religious Broadcasters conventions in Washington, 1983 marked the first time any president traveled outside Washington to speak to evangelicals. When he did, in Orlando on March 8, 1983, Reagan gave probably the most controversial, and surely most oft-quoted speech of his presidency.

Many commentators took umbrage when the president spoke not of a generic belief in God, but of his faith in the Lord Jesus. The *New York Times'* Anthony Lewis called his speech outrageous and primitive, terming his development of the reality of sin in the world "a simplistic theology—one in fact rejected by most theologians." Lewis failed to note the decline of such liberal theology and the parallel sway of evangelical theology.

It was Reagan's application of the doctrine of sin that produced the greatest apoplexy among his critics, for this was his "evil empire" speech. He stated that the Soviet Communists were "the focus of evil in the modern world," arguing that American military strength was necessary to restrain the "aggressive impulses of an evil empire." He pled for evangelicals to support his strong national defense and deterrence policies and to oppose voices calling for a nuclear freeze.

A STRING OF SUCCESSES

Evangelicals began getting into the game in earnest, wanting to change the political landscape by pressing their senators and representatives with letters, phone calls, and personal contacts. Small victories started to appear. In 1981, the Family Protection Act was introduced, designed to relieve some of the pressures imposed on families by government. One section or another of this omnibus pro-family bill would become law over the next several years.

The following year saw evangelical Dr. C. Everett Koop finally confirmed as surgeon general of the United States. Without the help of phone calls targeted at members of the Senate Labor and Human Resources Committee on Koop's behalf, his nomination might not have been ratified.

Thanks to a joint resolution passed by Congress, 1983 was signed into law by the president as the "Year of the Bible." Sen. Bill Armstrong (R-CO) gave strong leadership to achieving this national acknowledgment of the place of the Bible in America's heritage.

THE GREAT HARVEST OF 1984

Within a span of just a few weeks in the summer of 1984, evangelicals reaped a rich legislative harvest. Four important pieces of legislation at last bore fruit, each dating back at least three years.

DRUNK DRIVING LEGISLATION

For years Americans had inexplicably tolerated drunk driving, apparently not willing to face the reality of 25,000 annual alcohol-related traffic fatalities—almost a daily equivalent to the Air Florida crash of 1982.

Why the apathy? Why had nothing been done? Perhaps many lawmakers who drank realized they had often gotten away with driving under the influence, and that strong sentences one day might penalize themselves or their friends. We began to editorialize that evangelicals, two-thirds of whom are teetotalers, must take the lead on the issue. When the legislation passed, *Christianity Today* reported comments by a spokesman for Sen. Claiborne Pell (D-RI), chief sponsor of drunk driving legislation, that NAE's newsletter "generated a tremendous amount of mail" on the subject. Obviously, we were not the only ones.

CHURCH AUDIT PROCEDURES ACT

In 1981 Mike Coleman visited us in Washington. He and other leaders of the Gulf Coast Community Church in Mobile, Alabama, were troubled about an Internal Revenue Service investigation of their church. The IRS wasn't talking about the reasons for its probe, and eventually it went far beyond the bounds of propriety in making a brazen request to see all the pastor's personal counseling notes.

At the outset, the church was willing to cooperate, in the spirit of the biblical command to "submit yourselves for the Lord's sake to every authority instituted among men" (1 Peter 2:13). But the later demands were impossible. Everyone but the IRS understands that clergy confidentiality is traditionally as sacrosanct as a private lawyer-client relationship. By 1982, the church had finally cleared its name at a cost of more than $100,000 in legal and accounting fees. Not to mention the aggravation. Sadly, most of the expenditure could have been saved if the IRS had originally informed the church of the basis for its concerns. As it turned out, a disgruntled former member of the church had alleged that church funds were being used for private gain, and had submitted stolen papers as evidence.

Coleman's visit eventually led to the drafting of legislation to prevent future harassment of churches, conventions, or associations of churches. It defined the rights and responsibilities of churches in cooperating with IRS investigations, but also placed several requirements upon the IRS. On May 11, 1983, Rep. Mickey Edwards (R-OK) introduced the Church Audit Procedures Act in the House, and simultaneously Sen. Charles Grassley (R-IA) introduced his Senate version. The White House had to order its own Treasury Department not to oppose the bill. Through congressional committee testimonies, marshaling evangelical and other grass roots support, and contacts with members of Congress and their staffs, the CAP Act became the law of the land—attached to the must-pass Senate Deficit Reduction Act. There will be no more IRS "fishing expeditions" in evangelical churches, or in any others.

ALLEGED SOCIAL SECURITY TAX ON CHURCHES

Government economists realized, back in 1982, that Social Security was paying out $17,000 more per minute than it was taking in—a total calculated at nearly $9 billion per year. A National Commission on Social Security Reform was therefore appointed to stop the hemorrhage and to adjust the system for the long term. The president was alarmed enough to talk about a "pending insolvency."

When the commission made its report, it bundled together many provisions to increase revenues, including a requirement that all employees of nonprofit organizations be required to join. That meant churches would be included, not counting ordained ministers who had always been treated as self-employed for Social Security purposes. Paid church custodians, secretaries, organists, and the like would now come under Social Security. For the first time, churches were to be taxed with respect to their religious activity, as distinguished from unrelated business income. It was obvious from the beginning that this provision would never be deleted, because the commission had agreed that the bailout was a package, and that openness to change at any one point would cause their plan to fall apart.

Few evangelical churches voiced objections to the new tax. They saw it as a pass-through tax for the ultimate benefit of their employees, rather than an assessment upon the church itself. Several fundamentalist pastors, however, intensely protested. They felt that submitting to this tax would be equivalent to taking money given to the Lord and handing it over to Caesar. So adamant were they, that they spoke of chaining themselves to the White House gates in protest, and they seemed perfectly willing to go to jail for their convictions.

What better way to serve God and country than to head off a church-state confrontation. We asked Congress to accommodate the sincere religious beliefs of our fundamentalist friends. In a hearing before the Senate Finance Committee, an NAE proposal was built into the law, becoming an almost word-for-word solution to the problem.

Once again, evangelicals realized the value of grass roots complaints, even to the scheduling of a hearing. Ultimately, when the entire Social Security bailout package was adopted it included our provision to avoid church-state conflict. No minister would have to go to jail.

ACHIEVEMENTS IN THE 1990S

The federal government has a huge pot of alphabet soup perpetually simmering on its stove. So it's not easy to get excited about victories involving acronyms like ADA, ABC, and RFRA—until their meaning is spelled out.

THE AMERICANS WITH DISABILITIES ACT (ADA)

When the House joined the Senate in overwhelming approval of the Americans with Disabilities Act in the summer of 1990, one columnist wrote that the ADA was the "personal, daily equivalent of the fall of the Berlin Wall." Given that appraisal, only the grinch that stole Christmas might have opposed it.

Earlier, however, there was much to oppose. For one thing, an amendment excluding certain sexual behavior disorders from the bill had to be retained, lest churches be forced to hire against their religious belief. For another, churches had to be exempted from the public accommodations section of ADA, lest government treat them like hotels or shopping centers. That may require an explanation. Think of a typical old New England Church in a small village with its sanctuary on the second floor. The congregation of fifty can barely maintain the building and pay their pastor. If a "public accommodation," ADA could have forced that church to install an elevator it could not possibly afford, whether any disabled person might ever want to worship there or not. Government would be dictating to a church how it must spend "the Lord's money."

In the end, the religious grass roots were heard, changes were made in the two critical sections, and NAE's memo interpreting ADA could conclude that "The Act in principle requires no more of employers than the parable of the Good Samaritan." Unfortunately, intrusive courts may today be pushing private business beyond what the Samaritan demands.

THE ACT FOR BETTER CHILD CARE (ABC)

Working its way through Congress over several years, the Act for Better Childcare was sarcastically dubbed The Act for Bureaucratic Control by then Senate minority leader Bob Dole. Not as simple as ABC, the bill restricted parental choice, favored middle and upper income over lower income families, and discriminated against religious day-care centers and full-time homemakers. The prospect was that the federal government would become a sort of National Nanny. Evangelicals and other profamily forces favored a tax credit for child care as fairest for everyone concerned.

Just before adjournment in 1990, Congress passed a $24 billion five-year child care package, with over 75 percent of the funding going in earned income tax credits for low income parents. While most of the benefits went to families with both parents working outside the home, there was some funding for families where one parent chooses to stay home. Best of all, the bill's statutory language for the first time affirmed the right of parents to use child care vouchers in religiously-oriented programs of their own choosing.

However, we weren't finished yet. Sometimes regulations developed by bureaucrats undercut congressional intent. In this case, White House chief of staff John Sununu deserves credit for scheduling numerous meetings over several months, where profamily and religious organizations met with White House budget or health and human services personnel, to assure that religious aspects of the child care bill would not be lost. They weren't.

THE RELIGIOUS FREEDOM RESTORATION ACT (RFRA)

In the spring of 1990, the Supreme Court handed down a devastating decision in Oregon v. Smith. The new rule of constitutional law announced by the Court effectively gutted the Free Exercise Clause of the First Amendment. If prohibiting the exercise of religion is "merely the incidental effect of a generally applicable and otherwise valid provision," the Court held, "the First Amendment has not been offended." Until that decision, it was established law that government had to demonstrate a "compelling state interest" to justify applying a law that would burden an individual's free exercise of religion, and that it was using "the least restrictive means."

In short, because of the ominous consequences of this ruling, we helped develop and hold together one of the broadest coalitions ever seen on Capitol Hill to support corrective legislation, the Religious Freedom Restoration Act. Among others, it included the Christian Legal Society, the ACLU, the National Association of Evangelicals and the National Council of Churches, Concerned Women for America, and People for the American Way.

For more than three years hopes rose and sank with congressional schedules and strong opposition from some who should have been on our side from the first. Our broad coalition was reflected in the Senate cosponsors, liberal Ted Kennedy (D-MA) and conservative Orrin Hatch (R-UT). In the spring, major opposition collapsed; in October, the Senate passed RFRA 97-3 (months before, the House had done so on a voice vote); in November, the president signed RFRA into law in a White House ceremony.

Just how important was RFRA? No more momentous religious liberty legislation has become law since the adoption of the Bill of Rights, including the First Amendment. Without RFRA for example, churches whose beliefs do not allow the hiring of women as ministers or of homosexuals as youth workers might not have been able to defend a lawsuit on the basis of the Free Exercise Clause. Now they can.

Simply to mention other achievements is evidence enough that evangelicals were getting accustomed to the prospect of having a great influence on Congress and the White House. Nobody thought it could be done for the seventeenth consecutive year, given a one-party, pre-Gingrich government, but Congress again approved the Hyde Amendment, forbidding federal funding of abortions. President Clinton's pledge to open the military to homosexuals was repudiated by his own military leadership and by public opinion. When he backed down to a "don't ask, don't tell" policy, gays felt betrayed.

In 1991, Christian citizens played a major role in supporting the nomination of Judge Clarence Thomas to the Supreme Court. Toward the end of his administration, President George Bush bowed to the pressure, much of it from evangelicals, to fire National Endowment for the Arts director John Frohnmayer. A member of the cultural elite, he "never did get it" where the funding of blasphemous and obscene art was concerned.

THE MIRACLE OF EQUAL ACCESS

Anybody who does not perceive "the moral of the story" of Equal Access must be intellectually or spiritually challenged. It appears last in this chapter, even though it is one of four remarkable achievements from 1984.

In the *Widmar v. Vincent* decision of 1981, the Supreme Court ruled that a state university may not prevent campus organizations from conducting religious services on campus. A ban on religious worship would be a ban on free speech. It would be no violation of the Establishment Clause of the First Amendment to hold such forums in state university facilities.

Religious groups should have "equal access" to those facilities. The court indicated, however, that this decision pertained only to the collegiate level, and that it might rule differently regarding lower level students of "impressionable age."

The Christian Legal Society (CLS) and NAE were the original allies seeking equal access for high school students. It was ridiculous to think that, at their age, those students needed to be "protected" from discussions of religion, given their wide-ranging high school agendas, or that they might somehow be confused into thinking that a student-sponsored Bible club was state-sponsored because it met in their school building. It seemed that the only kind of speech discriminated against in public schools was religious speech. It was as if a sign was posted at the entrance to America's high schools:

ATTENTION STUDENTS
Your Bill of Rights Forbids
All Voluntary Religious Speech
Among Students in a Group of Two or More
Any Place on this Campus
at Any Time

We intended to establish the civil right to meet in student-initiated clubs "for the purposes of religious speech." CLS drew up a model Free Speech Protection Act, first introduced by Sen. Mark Hatfield (R-OR) before the Senate Judiciary Committee. Later his bill took on the name of equal access legislation, like that sponsored by Sen. Jeremiah Denton (R-AL). In the House, Rep. Don Bonker (D-WA) championed the cause. In the summer of 1983, CLS director Sam Ericsson and his staff were instrumental in winning the key legal case which would be at the heart of the battle for equal access, *Bender v. Williamsport* School District.

We did everything humanly possible to win passage of the Equal Access Act. CLS and NAE drew up more than twenty pages of questions and answers for members of Congress, so that they could anticipate every possible argument and have convincing answers for colleagues, the press, and the people back home. When the issue came into the courts, we filed friend-of-the-court briefs. Joined in progress by the Baptist Joint Committee on Public Affairs, we worked with the staffs of members.

When the issue reached the floor of the Senate and House, we helped produce a huge grass roots mail and telephone support on Capitol Hill. Especially important in that was Dr. James Dobson, who would invite one or another of us onto his "Focus on the Family" radio program to explain the issue. When he asked his listeners to call, they did, and his is the second most widely syndicated radio program in the nation.

At the end, when equal access had become law, we pulled together a consulting group to draft guidelines for interpreting and implementing the act—including former opponents such as the American Civil Liberties Union, the American Jewish Congress, the National Council of Churches, and even People for the American Way, all of whom had a vested interest in seeing that equal access be applied fairly. High school principals reading the guidelines are encouraged to find them clear and balanced, not mere propaganda published by "whining" religious groups.

Having worked to the maximum, all of us willingly admit that without God's providence, equal access would never have become law. Let me cite just three instances where it would demand more faith to think that we were "lucky" than to see God's hand at work.

First, at the heart of the battle was Lisa Bender, the Pennsylvania high school student who wanted to have a prayer club at Williamsport High School. Before the equal access concept got to Congress, she moved to Kentucky to train to be a missionary. Out of 435 congressional districts in the nation, she just "happened" to move into the district represented by the venerable Carl Perkins (D), chairman of the House Education and Labor Committee. Perkins took special interest in the legal battle of one of his constituents, and any education issue would necessarily pass through his committee.

Second, while the Senate quickly passed Equal Access 88-11, the House twice killed the bill. The day before equal access finally passed on July 25, a federal court of appeals turned thumbs down on the concept but, strangely enough, word of that decision did not reach Washington that day. Nor did it arrive the next day—until ten or fifteen minutes after the close of the 337-77 affirmative vote. The court's action might have turned the House vote around. Why did Congress not know about it in time? I say it respectfully and literally—God only knows.

Third, except for Rep. Perkins, equal access would never have reached the floor of the House that day. Perkins was so incensed by Speaker Tip O'Neill's blatant attempt to bury the bill that he threatened to bypass him with a rare parliamentary maneuver, the Calendar Wednesday procedure. An arcane rule allowed a committee chairman, on certain Wednesdays, to force a piece of legislation out of his committee and onto the floor of the House for a vote. Because such an action would be contrary to the will of the speaker, who otherwise would have cooperated with the chairman's wish, it would incur the speaker's wrath and sour their relationship for months or years to come. Thus, this tactic had been successfully employed just once in the prior quarter century. The speaker was sufficiently intimidated by Perkins that he capitulated. Equal access got another vote and passed.

That was Carl Perkin's final legislative victory. He was stricken with a fatal heart attack nine days later, on a flight home to his beloved Kentucky. God preserved his life until well into his seventy-second year. Equal access was his legacy.

As the equal access victory demonstrates, Christians must do everything humanly possible, at the same time committing the results to God. That's a formula for success in politics—and in all of life. When the Divine Will and human effort mesh, you have an irresistible force.

Anyone claiming that evangelicals won no significant political victories in Washington in recent years is either ignorant or bearing false witness. Remarkably, these successes came with the support of only a small percentage of the evangelical community.

What if hundreds of thousands of additional Christians had joined forces with the comparative handful then involved? What if you, your friends, and your church had been involved? Surely multiplied millions of evangelicals could be winning major, front-page victories in America's culture war.

But we haven't...yet!

WHAT

THE

CRISIS

INVOLVES

CAN WE CHANGE THE POLITICIANS' THINKING?

A pplause, mingled with boos and hisses, is about all the average voter is willing to contribute to public life."[1] If that statement is anywhere near reality, then evangelicals have a marvelous opportunity—but they must be above average in political smarts.

The Bible and history teach us that there are two ways by which Christians can change a society. When they fulfill their function as *light*, their nation can be *transformed through the spiritual processes of evangelizing and equipping*. When they fulfill their function as salt, their nation can be *reformed through the political processes of educating and electing*.

During the mid-twentieth century, fundamentalists became almost totally occupied with their role as light, while theological liberals majored almost exclusively on their responsibility to be salt. With Carl F. H. Henry's pivotal 1947 book *The Uneasy Conscience of Modern Fundamentalism* as a catalyst, evangelicalism's growing involvement in social and political concerns marked a distinction from fundamentalism.

Today, evangelical Christianity realizes that to be fully biblical, it must function as both salt and light. The twin goals of transforming and reforming are as essential as the two wings on an eagle, as necessary as two oars on a rowboat. Their evangelizing/ equipping and educating/electing functions are as indispensable as the two blades on a pair of scissors.

Hundreds of books have been written to motivate evangelicals to do evangelism and to equip the church's converts to be mature and responsible followers of Jesus Christ. What follows in this chapter and the next should provide down-to-earth assistance to those who want to reshape society through the political process.

Evangelicals must agree on two objectives. *Their short-range goal* must be *to change the politicians' thinking.* That is first done through educating themselves, and then persuasively educating their elected officials. Their *long-range goal* must be *to change the politicians themselves,* when their record in office reveals an unwillingness to change their voting. The latter, of course, is done through electing replacements and is the subject of the following chapter.

Evangelicals must rise to a new level of civic awareness. Hosea lamented the word of the Lord that warned, "My people are destroyed from lack of knowledge" (Hosea 4:6). Too many Christians are blank slates when it comes to the crucial issues of religious liberty and national morality, and they have generally adjusted to being informed only after the fact. Most often they have no one to help channel their concerns so that they actually influence lawmakers.

To remedy their political innocence, evangelicals must become readers in addition to being radio listeners and television viewers. A twice-weekly newspaper cannot be substituted for a major city daily newspaper, the *Wall Street Journal,* or even *USA Today.* The last is often criticized as the "fast food" newspaper, but it includes (albeit with short articles) broad coverage of the White House and Congress, stuff that many papers omit. *People* magazine is no substitute for a newsweekly. Knowledgeable citizens will read at least one of these magazines: *Time, Newsweek, U.S. News & World Report,* or the evangelical newcomer, *World.*

And books. The conventional wisdom says 10 percent of the people read 90 percent of the books. The simple fact is readers are leaders. That's why I suggest that one component of a successful church youth program should be to encourage the youth to become serious readers. In a 1990 survey, the Educational Testing Service concluded that only 40 percent of young Americans could read well enough to grasp the meaning of a typical newspaper column. If evangelicals are going to influence the nation, their high school generation must become a major segment of that intelligent minority.

On the Madison Building of the Library of Congress, these words of our fourth president are inscribed: "Knowledge shall forever govern ignorance. And a people who mean to be their own governors must arm themselves with the power which only knowledge gives."

GETTING INVOLVED IN A GROUP

Evangelical zeal, accompanied by knowledge rather than mere emotion, will lead Christians to influence their lawmakers in one or more of these ways: through single-interest groups, through groups with broader agendas, and through personal contact. Get on the mailing list of groups you respect, and heed their urgings to write or phone elected officials.

Pro-life, anti-pornography, or tax limitation groups are typical single-issue organizations. While they are often exceedingly effective, I offer one caution. Members must not assume that their one issue is the be-all and end-all of political involvement. They must constantly glance from side to side.

Multiple-interest groups include chambers of commerce, farm bureaus, teachers' unions, environmental clubs, religious organizations and the like—plus political parties. In local areas, groups may spring up with undefined names such as "Citizens for Better Government," whose purpose will need to be researched. It is not unthinkable that many readers of this book should initiate a citizen's group, recruiting concerned friends and neighbors to respond to a particular problem. "Parents for Traditional Values," for example, might focus on sex education in local schools.

At a White House briefing for religious leaders from around the country, Doug Wead, for two years President Bush's liaison to religious groups, warned that newcomers who wanted to influence the White House might, by trial and error, make a limited impact here or there. Instead, however, he recommended that they consider working through "the evangelical lobby" already in place in the capital. Several groups knew the ropes, he said, and could much more effectively help to channel their input.

Wead then listed just three groups, in this order: The National Association of Evangelicals, involved by far the longest and working on the broadest range of issues; Concerned Women for America, with a membership much larger than that of the National Organization for Women; and Focus on the Family's Family Research Council, the very effective and highly professional "new kid" on the block.

Whenever and however individuals channel their political energies, it will always be crucial for evangelicals to develop personal contact with those whom they have elected. There are two reasons for that. First, such contact is probably the most effective way of persuading, especially when reinforced by others feeling the same way. Members of Congress find the positions of most groups predictable, but letters on one issue from fifty voters in their district get their attention.

Second, and equally important, the church is clearly off the hook with respect to charges of improper religious influence when its individual members are the primary means of political participation. In other words, when the churches encourage *individual involvement rather than institutional involvement* in politics, nobody can properly criticize them—not constitutional lawyers, not hostile humanists, not super-critical media. Furthermore, the church does not become politicized.

For such an approach to work in any church, all that is necessary is agreement on the part of the church's leadership and a decision to provide reliable, nonpartisan, and relevant sources of information to the members.[2] Individuals may then respond to items especially interesting to them and, to state the obvious, the church in no way controls their input into political decision-making. This is not merely a beautiful theory. It works. When members of Congress receive such grass roots communications, they may not even realize they are being targeted as part of an orchestrated campaign. If they did, they might discount the importance of some of their mail.

AVOIDING FIVE COMMON MISTAKES

It's easy enough to destroy your effectiveness. Approach an irrelevant official, at an inappropriate time, with inaccurate information, using an inferior method, promoting an ill-advised idea and your credibility will soon disappear.

Irrelevant officials are those who can afford to overlook your opinions because they don't represent you. If you live in Illinois, a member of Congress from California could not care less about your views. So, get in touch with the two United States senators from your state and the one representative in Congress from the district where you live. As a voter, you will be deciding whether to retain or reject them in future elections. That's why they must pay attention to your views. There are just a few exceptions to this rule, such as a senator who may be running for president, or the speaker of the House, who must be concerned with his party's overall image.

The most *inappropriate time* is after the fact, subsequent to the final vote. Newspapers will give a sense of when members' time is becoming consumed with certain major issues. It might be well to postpone writing on your concern until congressional leadership begins to talk about taking up a certain bill. On the other hand, early-on voters may need to urge that an issue be included in the legislative agenda.

Inaccurate information is most unfortunate. How would you like to be an evangelical Congressman mistakenly charged with voting to support pornography? It happened to a friend. How would you like to be the Federal Communications Commission, receiving nearly 30 million unnecessary petitions in response to a phony rumor that atheist Madalyn Murray O'Hair is trying to remove all religious broadcasting from the air? That also happened, starting in the 1970s, and it hasn't stopped yet.

Inferior methods of communication to elected officials include group/form letters and pre-printed postcards. Members of Congress and their staff can sniff out obviously organized efforts, which have lower impact. I can testify to that personally, having received a four-inch pile of printed postcards when running for Congress. Without straining, my mind could easily picture one person working away at her kitchen table, with different colored pens and creative writing styles, signing twenty-five different names. To most politicians, one personally written letter is more influential than a whole stack of form letters or cards.

Ill-advised ideas are common enough. One angry constituent wrote a senator to ask that daylight savings time be rescinded, because the extra hour of sunlight was scorching his lawn. Many ideas sound great, until thought through. A bill to outlaw the portrayal of violence on television, once actually proposed, seemed worthy enough until it was pointed out that such a law would not only prohibit the showing of gratuitous violence, but also World War II newsreel footage or a dramatization of the crucifixion of Christ.

COMMUNICATING EFFECTIVELY

Those who wish to be effective in writing or phoning their members of Congress, the president, their governor, their state legislators, and others, will follow several tested guidelines:

• *Be correct.* Errors of name, etiquette, or spelling will diminish the impact of any letter. The proper forms for letters to Congress or the president are found in a footnote under Chapter 7 at the end of the book.[3]

• *Be courteous.* An honest element of appreciation at the beginning sets an excellent tone. Never threaten. Avoid harshness, anger, sarcasm, or a condescending tone. Don't become a nuisance as a regular "pen pal."

• *Be clear.* If letterhead is not used, provide a return address and a legible signature. Business or professional letterhead may impress, although care must be taken so that a businessman from New York City, for example, makes clear that he has written to a congressman from Connecticut where he resides. Refer to a specific bill by name and number if possible. State clearly what you want, whether asking him to cosponsor a bill, request a hearing, or vote a certain way.

• *Be concise.* A letter should deal with only one subject because it will be directed to a legislative assistant specializing in that issue. A second or third subject might be lost in office routing. An ideal letter will be one page long, although it might profitably enclose a persuasive column or article.

• *Be convincing.* Using your own words (staff will spot identical typed or handwritten copies of a "sample" letter suggested in a church bulletin), express yourself persuasively on why you feel strongly for or against your subject. In the process, you might even give a senator an argument she can use to win over colleagues or constituents.

• *Be constructive.* A writer who suggests how a bill could be amended to make it acceptable provides a great service to his officeholder. Ask for a reply, to be sure that your letter gets proper attention. If a congressperson votes according to your wishes, a thank-you note is always in order.

Telephone calls to your senators or representative need not be long distance. Senators will have several offices in their state, and a congressman will have one or more depending on the size of his district. The phone is especially useful when time is of the essence—for example, when there is a vote the next day. Calls will be tabulated and reported, but letters allow explanations rather than just yea or nay opinions. Generally, calls from strangers are not overly productive, so that the phone is a better tool when a member or staffer knows the caller.

Visits with members of Congress are sometimes possible in their Washington offices, by advance appointment. Many of the suggestions above concerning letter writing should be adapted for a visit. Instead of one page, you may be limited to ten minutes. Personal visits in your state or district are much more likely.

Almost any citizen who wants to do so can meet his senators and representative within the next six months. Read their mailings about town meetings or watch the papers for where they will speak. Go. Ask questions. Form a personal impression of them. You can become part of the tiny percentage of Americans who actually change the thinking of their elected officials.

Persuasive, well-reasoned letters to the editor and guest columns in local papers can also be effective. With the mushrooming of talk-radio shows, a cogently stated opinion can influence thousands of listeners.

Some people still ask the question, *"Do contacts with members of Congress make any difference?"* According to 219 top congressional staff members surveyed by the *Washingtonian* magazine in 1983 the answer is emphatically yes! The factors most influencing the decisions of the lawmakers were, in order of priority: 1) a member's political philosophy; 2) constituent opinion; 3) office mail; 4) the White House; 5) party leaders; 6) the press back home; 7) Washington lobbies; and 8) the national media.[4]

If you are inclined to be cynical, you might regard the first answer above as designed to impress, to be the "right" response. On the other hand, your cynicism would probably confirm the correctness of answers two and three above, since there is no loftier goal in many members' thinking than their own re-election. And to be re-elected, lawmakers must know what their people are thinking.

In May 1983, I testified before a Senate committee concerning President Reagan's constitutional amendment to allow prayer in schools. In an unusual move, Senator Orrin Hatch (R-UT) called me back to the microphone later that afternoon. He wanted to clarify the position of other segments of the religious community. He concluded by asking me to plead with Christians to write him and their senators, who "need to know" public sentiment on the matter of school prayer.

My evangelical brothers and sisters occasionally cause me heartburn—sometimes by their use of the Bible in the political arena, and other times by their attitudes in exerting pressure. Too often I have watched a Christian wave his Bible in the air at a committee hearing and embarrassingly call for a legislative body to enforce it. Where the Bible is concerned, the wisdom of attorney-theologian John Warwick Montgomery commends itself:

> Believers should strive to legislate all those socially valuable moral teachings of Scripture whose value can be meaningfully argued for in a pluralistic society. In such areas (e.g., right-to-life, equal pay for equal work, etc.) evangelicals must not engage in "Christian crusades," implying that it's "Christians vs. pagans," but should offer arguments on scientific, social, and ethical grounds potentially meaningful to the non-Christian. Even if unbelievers are not convinced, they can see that Christians are making their case on grounds which they themselves must confess to be legitimate in a pluralistic

society. Then, even though believers vote en bloc and pass the legislation, the non-Christian has no right to claim that an alien religion is being imposed on him.[5]

Evangelicals must not lose their distinct Christian witness as they operate in the political realm. Former Ohio State football coach Woody Hayes, an advocate of four-yards-and-a-cloud-of-dust ground control football, used to defend his style of play by observing, "When you put a football into the air three things can happen, and two of them aren't good."

Well, when you put evangelicals into the political game, three things can happen, and two of them aren't good either. Those evangelicals can lose, or they can win, or, in the process of winning a political battle they can lose their testimony. In the 1984 struggle over a Christian school in Nebraska, many so-called Christians hassled state legislators with repeated telephone calls from midnight to the wee hours of the morning. That same year, far too many other alleged Christians phoned Capitol Hill with the message that their senators were going to hell if they didn't vote for equal access in the public schools. Not only was that message unkind, it was unbiblical. It would be better for such persons to stay away from politics than to cast shadows on the name of Christ.

All political leaders should be treated Christianly. It is the right way, and more than that—it works. Bitterness is counterproductive in dealing with elected officials, from the president to city council. Here is my most memorable experience with bitterness.

WITH MADALYN MURRAY O'HAIR
ON TELEVISION

O'Hair is the aggressive atheist who played a significant role in removing devotional Bible reading from America's schools in 1963. Twenty years later, I one day received a last-minute request from CNN to appear on a national call-in show to debate Mrs. O'Hair about prayer in schools. By "coincidence," just before leaving, I met Bill Murray, O'Hair's son, at the airport. At that time he had come far enough to believe in God; later he would become a Christian.

When I arrived at the CNN studios in Atlanta I was introduced to Mrs. O'Hair. She treated me like dirt. As we moved onto the set, she sneered, "I'm going to destroy you out here."

Waiting for the show to start, I prayed silently. My only request was that God would help me to be Christ-like in my responses. I felt sure that viewers would later recall my attitudes more than my arguments. What I hadn't considered was that they would remember O'Hair's attitudes more than her arguments, as well.

The moderator, Sandy, allowed Madalyn to begin. She warmed up by referring to me as a member of the National Association of Religious Nuts. I listened as she flailed wildly at me and took coarse verbal swings at Christians everywhere. When my turn came, she butted in before I completed a single sentence and kept it up throughout the program. The names she used on the air were worse than anything I've ever been called, but she really vented her spleen when we went off the air for a commercial.

Viewers took note. The first bunch of callers directed considerable sympathy toward me. During the half-time break, I asked the moderator for the lead when we returned, since Madalyn had dominated the first half.

"Sandy," I said when we resumed, "I am in the unusual position of being able to bring personal greetings to Mrs. O'Hair from her son Bill, whom I met a little over three hours ago at Washington's National Airport. Our viewers might be fascinated to know why Bill Murray flew to the Capitol tonight. Tomorrow afternoon he hopes to testify before a House Judiciary subcommittee about prayer in schools. He wants to help undo the terrible wrong done when he was used by his mother, as a boy of fourteen, in a lawsuit to remove prayer and Bible reading from schools."

Madalyn was apoplectic. "He knows where the money is," she sputtered. "He's on the religious gravy train and he'll be tithing the proceeds to the atheists." The studio audience seemed unconvinced.

Before it was over, Sandy assumed the moral high ground and berated O'Hair for several minutes, accusing her of attacking me undeservedly, lacking the manners to give me the courtesy I had shown her, and committing several other misdemeanors. It was difficult to keep a smile off my face.

Leaving the studio, I offered my hand and a polite, "Good night, Mrs. O'Hair." Turning on her heel, she spat, "It was not." That night viewers saw the difference between the fruit of atheism and the fruit of the Spirit (Galatians 5:19-23). Without making reference to physical appearance, Madalyn Murray O'Hair is the ugliest person I have ever met. She is incensed when Christians suggest it, but why not pray right now for that pitiful woman?

WHAT DO EVANGELICALS WANT?

Over the years, I have sometimes spoken on the subject, "What evangelicals want in politics." Listeners are disarmed on discovering that evangelicals are not guilty of the recurring charge that they have no political agenda beyond a couple of personal morality issues. On a broad range of issues, evangelicals have been and will continue to influence politicians' thinking.

On our agenda are six social values principles. Rooted as they are in biblical truth, most evangelicals will unashamedly subscribe to them. Having said that, it is important to acknowledge that sincere believers may differ on how these principles may be realized when it comes to specific policy prescriptions.

To illustrate, let's assume that nearly all evangelicals concur that lifting the United States' national debt to a ceiling of $4.5 trillion (reached August 15, 1994) is a moral evil, and that biblical justice requires government to live more responsibly—that is, within its means. Failure to take steps to bring federal budgets into balance is thus irresponsible, unfairly burdening the next generation of Americans to pay interest on this generation's overspending. But, by what policy prescription shall we begin to discipline ourselves? Shall we take the medicine of higher taxes? Of significantly reduced spending? Or of a combination of increased revenues and spending cuts? Evangelicals will be found holding and vigorously defending each of these options.

The rest of this chapter could legitimately be expanded into an entire book. Thus, policy concerns mentioned under each principle are merely suggestive and not meant to imply a complete evangelical platform. Most are issues on which evangelicals have achieved consensus and acted, while others may yield consensus and authority to act in days to come. The principles themselves have been submitted as testimony to the platform committees of the Republican and Democratic National Conventions in years gone by.

• Preeminence of Religious Liberty

Religious liberty is the first liberty in the Bill of Rights, which in turn consists of the first ten amendments to the Constitution. That is fitting and proper for a God-given right, and so it is at the top of an evangelical agenda. If religious liberty can be restricted, reduced, or rescinded, then our basic right to protest government action is diminished.

"Proclaim liberty throughout the land" (Leviticus 25:10) is inscribed on the historic Liberty Bell in Philadelphia's Constitution Hall. For Christians, the ultimate importance of such freedom lies in Jesus' words, "You will know the truth, and the truth will set you free" (John 8:32). Without religious liberty, men and women can be deprived of the eternally important opportunity to consider the claims of Jesus Christ.

Government must not infringe upon religious freedom by entangling itself in the affairs of America's churches, synagogues, and religious schools. When I first came to Washington, evangelicals were troubled about the threat of H.R. 41. Introduced in the prior Congress out of concern for financial abuses among religious groups, it would have required churches and Christian organizations to report their contributors to the government. Fortunately, no such proposal is a threat today. The bill was shelved, partly because the Evangelical Council for Financial Accountability was developed to allow evangelicals to police themselves. No other segment of the religious community has a similar organization.

Thomas Jefferson said it best: "Eternal vigilance is the price of liberty." That being the case, evangelicals often join friend-of-

152 Stand and Be Counted

the-court briefs for unpopular religious groups, or form broad and otherwise unlikely coalitions to defend religious liberty. Nonetheless, that liberty is in jeopardy in our culture. The leader of the Christian Legal Society wrote of these frightening realities: "We can more freely hand out condoms in schools than religious tracts. Acceptance of sodomy can be taught, but the Ten Commandments cannot be displayed on the public school wall. And public school teachers can refer students to abortion clinics, but they cannot invite students to church."

• Profession of Public Faith in God

On April 30, 1789, George Washington placed his hand on an open Bible on the balcony of Federal Hall in New York City and repeated the oath of office prescribed in the Constitution.

> Then, after pausing briefly, Washington electrified the hushed crowd by adding his own words: "I swear, so help me God." A murmur spread through the crowd and the inaugural party. This was not part of the oath of office, although the precedent set by Washington has been followed by every president since. Then Washington bent over and kissed the Bible. Another murmur. Judge Livingston turned to the thousands below and cried out: "Long live George Washington, President of the United States!" The people cheered, church bells rang, and cannons fired.[6]

Simply put, America historically has acknowledged God's existence and his sovereignty. Evangelicals are grateful for that, believing that "blessed is the nation whose God is the LORD" (Psalm 33:12). In the dark days of the Civil War, President Lincoln designated a day in April 1863 as a national day of prayer. Here is the opening statement of his proclamation:

> Whereas the Senate of the United States, devoutly recognizing the Supreme Authority and just government of Almighty God in all the affairs of men and nations, has, by a resolution, requested the President to designate and set apart a day for national prayer and humiliation; and whereas it is the duty of nations, as well as of men, to own their dependence upon the overruling power of God, to confess their sins and transgressions in humble sorrow, yet with assured hope, that genuine repentance will lead to mercy and pardon, and to recognize the sublime truth announced in the Holy Scriptures, and proven by all history, that those nations only are blessed whose God is the Lord.[7]

On July 11, 1955, Congress passed a bill to place the inscription "In God We Trust" on all currency and coins. On July 3 the following year, President Eisenhower signed into law a bill making "In God We Trust" the United States' national motto.

Evangelicals believe that national recognition of "the God who is there," to use Francis Schaeffer's memorable phrase, is essential for the blessing of the Lord of history. That acknowledgment is symbolized in the military chaplaincy, national days of prayer, and such a specific resolution as Congress' declaring 1983 to be "The Year of the Bible."

Czech President Vaclav Havel's Fourth of July 1994 speech in Philadelphia resounded with conviction, coming as it did from one who had lived under a terribly oppressive system and had been imprisoned for expressing his views: "The Declaration of Independence," he said, "states that the Creator gave man the right to liberty. It seems man can realize that liberty only if he does not forget the One who endowed him with it." Yet, in an American public school classroom today, a teacher making a similar statement can expect to be threatened with the loss of her job.

• Protection of Life as Sacred

Statistically, the most dangerous place to be in America is in a mother's womb. Abortion, not many years ago regarded as contradictory to a doctor's commitment to save life, is the most commonly performed surgical procedure today. In fact, the 28 million abortions performed in this country since 1973 equal the combined populations of the following states: Arkansas, Colorado, Iowa, Idaho, Minnesota, Missouri, Montana, Nebraska, North Dakota, Oregon, South Dakota, Utah, and Wyoming.[8]

Evangelicals are more nearly unanimous in opposing the surpassing moral evil of abortion-on-demand than on any other issue except homosexuality, and rightly so. Human beings are the culmination of creation, "made in the image of God" (Genesis 1:26-27), and thus able to have fellowship with God. Note that "there are six things the LORD hates, seven that are detestable to him," among which are "hands that shed innocent blood" (Proverbs 6:16-17). The fact that evangelical conviction on this practice is religiously based does not matter. In American politics, the source of an idea makes no difference whatever. It may arise from religion, a brainstorm, or a television docudrama. The legitimacy of the idea is established through reasoned debate and rests on its content.

Many politicians voting "pro-choice" claim they are "personally opposed" to abortion. But how, in the name of reason, can one find a practice immoral and not be publicly opposed to it? Would anyone respect a late twentieth-century argument that "While I am personally opposed to slavery, I feel I should not force my views on others?" To the contention that "a woman has the right to control her own body," we answer dryly, "Once you are pregnant, we're talking about two bodies." Americans love the freedom to choose, so pro-abortionists hammer on the theme of a woman's right of choice. Fine, but nobody I know boasts of being pro-choice on racial discrimination. Then why is it considered legitimate to take the life of a yet-to-be-born child?

Americans are living with contradiction about abortion. In one poll, 60 percent said that a woman should have the right to choose an abortion, while 70 percent said the unborn should be protected. Thirty-seven percent answered yes to both questions. The fact is that the majority of Americans oppose the majority of abortions—those done because birth control failed (about half), because a potential birth would be inconvenient, or for sex selection.

The sanctity of life is not just a birth issue. Evangelicals will never accept euthanasia (so-called "mercy killing"), although there will be legitimate debate about artificially extending the process of dying and about a clear definition of when death occurs. The nation must reverse the situation where decisions are made with an ambiguous and subjective "quality of life" standard, rather than "sanctity of life" as a clear and compelling one.

It took decades for this nation to conclude that slavery was evil. However long it takes to convince the United States that abortion is evil, evangelicals will stay in the battle.

• Provision of Justice for All

Evangelicals wholeheartedly conclude their pledge of allegiance to the flag with the phrase "...and justice for all." That reflects perfectly the character of the Creator, who reveals himself as a just God and who has said, "Let justice roll on like a river, righteousness like a never-failing stream" (Amos 5:24). Charles Colson points out that the biblical word *justice* is misunderstood if we think only of its secular definition: getting one's due. Rather, the word means "righteousness," as in the parallel clauses in Amos. Colson writes that our call to justice is "to bring the Lord's righteousness to individuals and the structures of society."[9]

Justice to the poor? Our biblical instructions could not be more clear. "Defend the cause of the weak and fatherless; maintain the rights of the poor and oppressed. Rescue the weak and needy; deliver them from the hand of the wicked" (Psalm 82:3-4). Willingness to vote the largest sums of money for poverty programs may not necessarily mark obedience to God's will. It is reported that we have invested more than $5 trillion in fighting poverty, yet a welfare expert at the Heritage Foundation reports: "The official poverty rate has remained largely unchanged since the War on Poverty began [during Lyndon Johnson's presidency], while the problems of family breakup, welfare dependency, eroded work ethic, and crime all have gotten dramatically worse."[10]

Government may have had good intentions, but the consequence of much of its welfare policy is tragic. Those who want to deliver the needy must create and help the poor to find jobs, enabling them to escape the dependent underclass. Aid to Families with Dependent Children (AFDC), to mention one badly flawed program, spurs the breakdown of the family by discouraging marriage, rewarding out-of-wedlock childbearing, and financially penalizing the single parent who takes a job. In short, AFDC subsidizes illegitimacy while marriage and work are taxed. It is not easy to change such policies, but it must be done for the poor to experience justice. They must be empowered to escape dependency, although their great temptation was once expressed by George Bernard Shaw: "A government which robs Peter to pay Paul can always depend on the support of Paul."

Reaction to injustice can produce an equally unacceptable reverse injustice, as in a case involving the Virginia Employment Commission. It rigged civil service test percentiles entirely on the basis of race, to give certain racial minorities a huge advantage over other test-takers.[11] What ever happened to justice for all?

In 1993, 27 percent of American children were living with one parent, twice as many as in 1970. That year, more than $34 billion in child-support payments went uncollected, 90 percent of that from deadbeat dads.[12] Justice demands that absentee fathers be forced to accept their court-assigned responsibilities, but of 23 million kids entitled to support, 80 percent receive none.

Justice demands many things: that the criminal justice system be reformed to reflect biblical values;[13] that the guilty not so often walk free while the innocent cower, terrified, in their homes; that victims' rights not be ignored when justice is served; that AIDS not be a politically protected disease; that parents, through tax credits or vouchers, be able to educate their children in the schools of their choice, whether public or private, rather than being economically forced to send them to a government monopoly school which undercuts their values; that taxes be increased significantly on alcoholic beverages and cigarettes, since their use costs society far more than even the highest current revenue proposals would return; that our young be protected from child abuse; that our courts' trial lawyers and juries cease labeling criminals "victims in need of healing," ultimately finding no one guilty of transgressing society's moral order or of sinning against God himself. There is no end to such a list of concerns, if there is to be justice for all.

PRESERVATION OF THE
TRADITIONAL FAMILY

Evangelicals must not capitulate to the sinister agenda of social engineers who, given vaguely written legislation, would assume functions that families should fulfill—indeed, functions assigned to the family by God. Above all, government policies must not usurp parental authority and responsibility for the decisions of minor children as, for example, in allowing abortion without parental consent. The biblical assignment is clear: "These commandments that I give you today are to be upon your hearts. Impress them on your children. Talk about them when you sit at home and when you walk along the road..." (Deuteronomy 6:6-7), and "If anyone does not provide for his relatives, and especially for his immediate family, he has denied the faith and is worse than an unbeliever" (1 Timothy 5:8).

Historically the family has been the cornerstone of American society. This fundamental building block has been composed of a married man and woman who have transmitted moral values to their children—not any miscellaneous conglomeration sharing a kitchen for more than three weeks. For most of our history, promiscuity was recognized as a threat to family life, and evangelicals and millions of others will always regard it so. Thus, there is an awful sense of foreboding today, with pornography a widespread plague, heterosexual purity an anachronism, and homosexuals blatantly flaunting their lifestyles and seeking to have their relationships and practices legitimized by government.

Illegitimacy is "an unprecedented catastrophe" according to *Washington Post* columnist David Broder.[14] Vice President Dan Quayle was pilloried by the media elite for knocking feminists' smug assurance that one-parent families are just fine, thank you, in the "Murphy Brown" episode during the 1992 campaign. The tune has changed, however, since the appearance of *Atlantic* magazine's lengthy cover article in April 1993, entitled "Dan Quayle Was Right." Since then, I have personally heard President Clinton deplore out-of-wedlock births, in the process approving Quayle's argument. The effect on males is equally sobering. More and more sociologists are pointing to young, unattached males as the cause for a highly disproportionate share of social ills. It can no longer be questioned that illegitimacy is the surest route to social decay and poverty. Yet 1993 Census Bureau figures show that children living with one parent are almost equally divided between children of divorce and children of a never-married woman and an irresponsible, unattached male.

Shifting tax policies have penalized families severely. In 1960, 60 percent of federal revenues came from individuals and families, with corporations providing 23 percent. By 1985, the business share had shrunk to 8.5 percent, while revenues from families and individuals had ballooned to 81 percent. To put it another way, in 1948 the average family of four paid just 2 percent of its total income in federal taxes; by the late eighties, that same family was turning over 24 percent of its income to the federal government. Rep. Henry Hyde (R-IL) points out that today's personal income tax exemption, if proportional to family income in 1948, would amount to about $8,000, not $2,350.[15]

Child care legislation advanced by Congress in the 101st Congress was seriously flawed because it discriminated against a full range of parental choice, including religious day-care services and families where one parent forgoes income from the market-place to rear children at home.

There is a large bundle of policies that come under the umbrella of "pro-family" issues. Evangelicals will be found fighting for those policies for years to come. Eternal vigilance is imperative.

• Promotion of Judeo-Christian Values in Education and Legislation

Columnist William Raspberry put his finger on the problem: "Almost too late, there seems to be developing a consensus that we'd better get busy teaching our children moral values...*somebody* ought to be teaching our children right from wrong—building their character."[16]

The *Wall Street Journal* reported that, in a 1990 survey, 84 percent of public school parents want moral values taught in school, while most teachers shy away from that assignment. Educational horror stories like the following seem incredible. A high schooler returning a lost bank bag with thousands of dollars in it is mocked by classmates as a fool. After discussion, his teacher refuses to say whether the honest student did the right thing or not, rationalizing, "I have no right to push my moral values on the students." But education cannot be value-neutral. In this instance, neutrality supports immorality by refusing to condemn dishonesty.

Students are pathetically left with moral ambiguity. Jack Kemp cited a *New York Times* interview with a seventeen-year-old California high school student who was arrested for rape and sexual harassment.[17] "They pass out condoms, teach sex education and pregnancy-this and pregnancy-that.... But they don't teach us any rules." Kemp labels the ethical relativism of our times as "a crisis of confidence in our own ideals...the strip-mining of our public spirit."

The loss of our moral consensus as a nation will ultimately cause our Republic to crumble. The Bible states: "Where there is no revelation, the people cast off restraint" (Proverbs 29:18). It is impossible to describe today's American society more perceptively than that. Fewer and fewer possess knowledge of biblical teaching or embrace its individual and national standards as authoritative.

Is it likely that we can restore Judeo-Christian values to education? Long-time congressman and then governor of Minnesota Al Quie once recounted to me his frustration on this score. His blue-ribbon governor's committee was assigned the task of devising a way to teach values in Minnesota's public school system. The committee sought to draw up a list of commonly accepted values that could be taught without reference to religion. When Quie suggested the word *fidelity* for the list, his own committee turned their governor down. Why? The word "sounded too religious." Imagine rejecting a strong value like fidelity, a word pertinent to keeping contracts or marriage vows. The incident symbolizes the titanic struggle over values in our society.

Right and wrong are being stood on their heads. Homosexuality is celebrated as virtuous because it is a radical expression of human freedom. The ACLU battles to prohibit advocating chastity in a sex education curriculum because it can only be a religious teaching. Members of Congress only slap the wrist of a fellow member guilty of flagrant immorality and illegal actions, and voters continue to return to office a representative who was censured for seducing an under-age House page.

America's traditional values are essential to make democracy and a free economy succeed. Yet those values are often hard to come by in Congress, the White House, governors' mansions, and state legislatures. Evangelicals have their short-range assignment cut out for them—to change their politicians' thinking.

CHANGING
THE POLITICIANS
THEMSELVES

D espite constant grass roots efforts, some politicians will prove impossibly stubborn when it comes to certain issues. Their minds simply will not be changed. Fortunately, we need not be perpetually frustrated when, for example, a senator's voting record shows that he inevitably prefers a woman's "right" to an abortion over protecting the unborn. Nor are we limited to gnashing our teeth when a congresswoman's vote reveals that she gives higher priority to gay rights than to a church's right to practice its faith.

Under the Constitution, when we are unable to change our office-holders' minds, we can change the politicians themselves. And doing that, through elections, is not as difficult as most people think. But it would be a whole lot easier if more citizens were willing to get involved.

It usually surprises people when they learn that our nation's political course has often swung on narrowly decided elections. Did you know that Richard Nixon came very close to defeating John F. Kennedy for the presidency in 1960? Or that Jimmy

Carter just barely turned Gerald Ford out of the White House in 1976?

Since we can never know in advance when our state or congressional district vote may be very close, our interests can be defeated by the narrowest of margins. The way to prevent that is by significant, personal campaign involvement. By the way, "significant" campaigning, for folks just starting, could be something as simple as putting a bumper sticker on their car. It could also be "significantly" more than that—and easy to do, fun, and of great consequence.

Who wins elections? The most attractive candidates? The candidates whose political views make the most sense? The candidates with the largest campaign treasuries? The answer is: None of the above.

SECONDARY FACTORS IN WINNING ELECTIONS

Appealing and articulate candidates with engaging personalities have no automatic lock on election victories. If you haven't sat recently in the gallery with the full House of Representatives in session, look through the *Almanac of American Politics* at the pictures of the members of Congress. Few of the men resemble Robert Redford, and few of the women beauty contest winners. But then, few of the general population would either. Those ordinary people who win elections are a cross section of the rest of us. You might even wonder how some of them could win with their strange-sounding names, some practically impossible to spell. No, the victors are not all a public relations firm's packaging dream.

Intelligent candidates, with a solid grasp of the issues and a good, commonsense political approach do not necessarily emerge victorious either. Some incumbents get away with voting one way in Washington and talking another way at home. Most citizens haven't the foggiest notion of the true voting record of their representatives or senators, and thus can easily have the wool pulled over their eyes. Further, the picture of a voting public eagerly standing by to throw bodily into office the candidate with genuine wisdom is too ludicrous to discuss.

Nor are affluent candidates necessarily guaranteed victory, whether personally wealthy or successful in fund-raising. In Wisconsin in 1980, former congressman Robert Kasten found himself in a three-way primary battle for the Republican nomination for the United States Senate. One of his opponents raised and spent $700,000. Another amassed an incredible (for 1983) $1.3 million. Kasten, however, won the nomination with campaign expenditures of only $70,000, and went on to win the Senate seat in November.

One rare exception to the minimizing of money should be noted. On occasion, a party cannot find a viable, willing challenger, yet wishes to field an opponent to the incumbent. That happened in 1990 when new York Governor Mario Cuomo seemed invincible. Republican leaders then "gave" the nomination to a politically unknown Pierre Rinfret, largely because he was willing to pour large amounts of his personal wealth into what others saw as a kamikaze run against Cuomo.

Don't misunderstand. Being attractive, astute, and affluent are not disadvantages for a political candidate. Conversely, there is no special advantage in being lackluster, stupid, or impoverished. Something else is almost invariably the key to success. It's organization.

THE NAME OF THE GAME

Other things being equal, the candidate backed by the best organization of volunteers is far more often than not going to win.
Evangelicals with experience in the work of the church should be
ahead of the game here. The parallel in methodology is remarkable. Churches that rely on an outstanding preacher to produce
growth, rather than organizing volunteers for the work of the
ministry, are not likely to set the ecclesiastical world on fire. And
political campaigns relying mostly on the exceptional qualities of
their candidate, no matter how outstanding, are not going to put
him in office without a strong corps of volunteers.

Bob Kasten took a lot of bows while in the Senate, because
his organizational strategy for victory had become legendary.
Professional campaign training seminars teach "The Kasten
Plan." For his congressional races, Kasten built a campaign organization with a traditional chairman and manager at the top.
Dividing his district into regions, his staff produced hundreds of
volunteers with a Kasten chairperson in every precinct. These
vital units, precincts, are as basic to the body politic as cells are to
the human body. County election officials arbitrarily draw up
precincts according to the number of voting-age citizens in each
area. Every precinct has a polling place for elections and serves as
a clearly defined area for political operations.

After careful analysis of the voting records, Kasten's campaign set a challenging but realistic goal for each precinct, and it
was each volunteer's responsibility to bring in that many votes or
more. Hundreds of men and women accepted the responsibility
to put Kasten into office, did what was necessary to "sell" voters
on their man, identified Kasten supporters, and one way or
another got them to the polls on Election Day. Their combined
efforts put him over the top.

No wonder, then, that in 1980 Kasten took his party's Senate nomination in spite of one of his opponents spending nineteen times the money he did, and the other ten times. Ironically, in the years between his service in the House and his entry into the Senate, Kasten ran for governor of Wisconsin and was defeated. In that one gubernatorial primary, the decision was made to short-cut his own strategy. Only once did Kasten not use his own "Kasten Plan," and that time he lost.

Incidentally, when it comes to elections, two kinds of organizations combine to assist candidates: political parties and the candidate's own campaign.

Always in place are the two national parties, with state, county, and local organizational structures. Each has a logical assignment: The national party to elect a president every four years; the state organization to elect statewide candidates to be governor, attorney general, U.S. senators and the like; the county party to elect county commissioners; and so on. Parties are comprised of an organization of officers and leaders, elected officials, grass roots activists who give time and money, and voters who identify with that party and generally support its candidates.

The other organization is the one developed by the candidate. It is always wise to build one's own organization, rather than to rely solely on the party. Deliberately or unconsciously, party workers may put more effort into another race. They may go all out for a glamorous gubernatorial nominee, but give only half-hearted effort to their steady congressional nominee. On the other hand, it would be a foolish candidate who did not cultivate party leaders warmly, letting it be known that he values party support as crucial for his campaign. And his volunteers, he will in turn promise them, always stand ready to help the party.

Early in 1975, a member of Congress told me that just three

hundred supporters, deeply committed to my campaign, would be enough to put me into Congress. I came home from my exploratory visit to Washington riding high. The sermon I heard the next Sunday was preached from the Old Testament account of a judge named Gideon (Judges 7). Because God did not want Israel to congratulate herself that her superior military might had won the victory over Midian, he instructed Gideon to send home any who were fearful. His force of 32,000 was reduced to 10,000, and then in a second step to a meager 300. Using God's strategy, that tiny band routed a superior Midianite army.

Hmmm. Three hundred to win a battle. Three hundred to put someone into Congress. Sermon application came easily that day. I slipped a note to Lynne. "We're going to build a committee of 300." She nodded and smiled.

We recruited many friends who had never before participated in a political campaign, always outlining the sort of work that would be required in the final weeks, and the kind of commitment we were counting on. Slowly we built the list, never adding names just to reach the magic number.

Our campaign manager was thrilled to see a list like that. He promptly mailed a letter to our committee, describing ways they could help and asking that a questionnaire be returned. When the response was disappointingly slim, Lynne volunteered to call everyone on the list who had not yet responded. Before the campaign was over, she called through that list four times. Not even the candidate's wife could prod most of those friends into meaningful action.

For whatever reasons, our committee of three hundred was mostly a paper committee, about one-third that size when it came to campaigning. The majority of our "committed" friends found no convenient time to give us a hand, or no suitable assignment. That wasn't for lack of options, however. Volunteers were needed to staff our office, put in some evenings on our telephone bank, spend a couple of Saturday mornings walking precincts with our literature, hold a coffee for me to meet their neighbors, and certainly write a check to the campaign.

If any one factor was responsible for my loss, beyond my shortcomings as a candidate, it was the failure of our campaign organization to live up to its potential. Other evangelical candidates have reported similar problems.

In contrast to my newcomer approach, here's the more common route to political office. In 1964, a young Denver area businessman's presidential preference was strong enough that he placed a political poster in a window. As he was cutting his grass one Saturday morning, a passing driver saw the sign, hit his brakes, rolled down his window, and commented about the Goldwater poster. In the ensuing conversation, he ruefully reported that Republicans hadn't been able to staff that precinct, and wondered if this new acquaintance might be willing to help. Never involved in politics before, Ted agreed to help, provided that he could have some guidance. He soon learned the ropes.

A couple of years later, Ted walked into his legislative district assembly a few minutes late. Suddenly there was silence and everyone looked at him. The chairman cleared his throat and took the plunge: "Ted, we've just been talking about you. As you know, nobody's come forward to run for the state legislature in this district. You've done a good job for the party in your precinct, we think you'd be a good candidate, and we frankly want you to run. How about it?"

Startled, Ted said precisely what most of us would have said: "Who, me?" That was the beginning. As an evangelical Christian, Ted prayed for God's leading in his decision—and it put him in the state legislature that year, even though his district's party registration was two-to-one against him. From there, he moved up to the state Senate where he served many years as Senate president, one of the most important positions in Colorado politics. Moreover, in 1978 and 1986 he won the GOP nomination for governor.

If Ted Strickland had refused to do basic precinct work in 1964, today only his family might know him in Colorado. Ted's willingness to invest a few hours in politics when he was young opened the door for him to run twice for governor, and to be one of Colorado's prominent political leaders.

It isn't surprising in the least that both Democrats and Republicans produce candidates from within their own ranks. The cream rises to the top in each party. Friendships, IOUs, and a certain logical progression make it possible for party insiders to predict who are likely to come along as nominees for the next decade. You can almost see the line forming. It is so unusual for a party to look beyond its own ranks to find a candidate that very few examples come to mind. Here's one. After World War II, both parties sought to cultivate war hero General Dwight Eisenhower as a presidential candidate. The Republicans snared him and thus controlled the White House for the following eight years.

The exception proves the rule. If evangelicals are disheartened that comparatively few fellow believers are in office, they should ask how many of their people are so involved in party politics that they, like Ted Strickland, might one day be running for governor. How many serve in the state legislature or as party county chairmen from which they are well positioned to run for Congress? Evangelicals, like anybody else, need to earn the right to ask their party to entrust them with a nomination for high office.

There's a lot to be learned from a quick look at some fascinating presidential and congressional election statistics. These are
not boring numbers. For those who care about change, they
make a powerful case for political involvement.

PRESIDENTIAL ELECTIONS

Because the three presidential elections of the 1980s were about
as one-sided as an earthquake, most Americans do not realize
that in several prior elections this century, the winners came close
to being defeated.

In 1976 Jimmy Carter defeated Gerald Ford by an electoral
vote of 297-240, but if Ford had carried Ohio with its twenty-
five votes (at that time), and Hawaii with its four, he would have
won by a hair's breadth—269-268. Such figures would be statistically meaningless except for the close margins in both of those
states. It would have required less than 5,600 switched votes in
Ohio and 3,700 in Hawaii to reverse the national outcome,
allowing Ford to remain as president.

Richard Nixon became president in 1968 with a popular
vote edge of only 510,000 out of 72 million votes cast, although
his electoral college margin was substantial. Of course, it is theo-
retically possible to win the presidency in the electoral college
while losing the popular vote. The more interesting Nixon election, statistically, was his loss eight years earlier to John F.
Kennedy. The 1960 electoral vote was 303-219.

If, however, Illinois and Missouri had gone Nixon's way, plus
any one of Nevada, New Mexico, or South Carolina, Kennedy
would have lost by at least 260-262 or a slightly higher margin.
Again, such speculation would mean little, except for the close
votes in all those states. Less than six thousand needed to be
switched in Illinois, where Chicago Mayor Richard Daley's

famed Democratic machine saw to it that the tombstones voted, early and often. In Missouri, less than five thousand needed to shift. With under thirteen hundred shifting in Nevada, less than twelve hundred shifting in New Mexico, or less than five thousand shifting in South Carolina, Nixon would have picked up the added three, four, or eight electoral votes necessary to put him over the top.

In 1916, before the days of computer projections, the nation waited much, much longer for ballots to be tabulated. Finally, it came down to California. If that West Coast state had gone Republican, former New York governor and associate justice of the Supreme Court, Charles Evans Hughes would have become president (instead of later returning to the Supreme Court in 1930 as chief justice). As it was, by that one state margin, Woodrow Wilson became president during World War I, assuming the weighty responsibilities of conducting the war and developing post-war policies.

In any or all of those elections, if the losing party had a gifted forecaster, it would have been no trick at all to rush reinforcements into the key states, pick up a few thousand votes, and turn the election around. Since only God has foreknowledge and omniscience, however, the parties must be guided by polling data, applying extra pressure in close states in hopes that the organizations will do their absolute best. That best is dependent on the hard work of volunteers.

Now for a candid question. Have evangelicals historically been much of a factor in the presidential campaign process?

For the most recent five elections, the answer is yes, but for decades of elections preceding 1976, the answer is no. While no political or church leader can create or control an evangelical voting bloc, nevertheless millions of evangelical Christians have collectively produced such a bloc by tracking certain issues, studying the parties, looking over the candidates, and voting accordingly. It began back in 1976, when evangelicals played the major part in putting "born again" Jimmy Carter into the Oval Office.

However, by 1980 many of those evangelicals had deserted the Southern Baptist president from Plains, Georgia, giving Ronald Reagan 61 percent of their vote to Jimmy Carter's 34 percent. The Reagan-Bush team did not forget their 1980 evangelical supporters as they looked toward '84. When 52.6 percent of Americans of voting age cast their ballots—reversing a declining presidential turnout of twenty years—Ronald Reagan ran up 525 electoral votes, the highest total ever.[1] CBS exit polls indicated that 78 percent of the white evangelical vote had helped Reagan build the fifth largest popular vote margin in history.

This second consecutive Republican victory prompted Rep. Pat Schroeder (D-CO) to suggest in a speech, "There are three things we Democrats need to do to recapture the White House." Pausing for effect, she finished, "Unfortunately, nobody knows what they are." The party's new national chairman had an idea for one smart step. He yanked official standing from the Gay and Lesbian Caucus—one among several glaring examples that Democrats were not seeking the evangelical vote in 1984.

Evangelical religious broadcaster Pat Robertson sought the Republican presidential nomination in 1988. While his showing was significant, and while he helped to focus the debate, he was never able to capture the evangelical community as his base, let alone find substantial support elsewhere. The media generally expressed surprise on learning that, in soundings of evangelical leadership, the NAE several times found Robertson only the fourth choice among Republican contenders. Many felt that his campaign was just not feasible—that America would not put an ordained minister in the Oval Office, even if he had turned back his ordination credentials. Others were uncomfortable with some of Robertson's theology or public utterances.

Before and after winning the Republican nomination, George Bush cultivated evangelical leaders in a number of small meetings in the nation's Capitol, some in his White House office, and others at his vice presidential residence. He listened to their counsel, echoed many of their convictions in his convention acceptance speech in New Orleans, and pulled 81 percent of the white evangelical vote in his near-landslide electoral college victory of 426-112. Evangelicals were the identifiable voting bloc which gave the largest percentage of its votes to Bush.

In a White House meeting a month later, I told the president-elect why I thought he had won such a victory: While his campaign train ran on the track of peace and prosperity, there was a third rail, as in Washington's Metro subway that delivered the power. That rail was traditional values. Not only evangelicals, but millions of others found those values appealing.

That summer, evangelical leaders had recommended three possible vice presidential choices that would send the right signal to their people: Senator Bill Armstrong of Colorado, Congressman Jack Kemp of New York, or Governor John Ashcroft of Missouri. The choice of Indiana Senator Dan Quayle took everyone by surprise, but evangelicals' immediate reaction was positive. Quayle held their value system and shared their faith. As the media pummeled Dan Quayle unmercifully, the Christian news magazine *World* ran this little piece in an article about him:

> He struggled with his grades from the day he entered school. He carried the rap of a pam-

pered child past from the time he was no longer
one. Even in his majority his mother did everything she could to see her son avoid exposure to
military action; when it was unavoidable, she
made certain he went in style. He rode off to
war as a correspondent in as much splendor as
a troopship could afford.... His valet even
packed a high powered spyglass for viewing the
battles from a safe distance.

His heroics on the battlefield were unofficial, tinted with a shade of circumstance and his
own embellishments. Returning from the battlefield, he enjoyed only fleeting glory and pop-
ularity, and was treated mercilessly by his peers
in the House of Commons.

But privilege, where it has touched on military experience, existed long before Winston
Churchill headed off to cover the Boer War.[2]

I do not assume that Dan Quayle would develop into a
Winston Churchill. Nor did I think the media should assume,
based on his early life, that he would not. In any case, by their
overwhelming vote, evangelicals put him into office along with
the forty-first president of the United States, George Herbert
Walker Bush.

President Bush enjoyed all-time approval ratings during the
Persian Gulf War, causing several top potential Democratic challengers to announce they would not seek the nomination in
1992. Political approval is ephemeral, however, and a number of

second-tier Democratic contenders took heart when Bush's ratings tumbled. Arkansas Governor Bill Clinton won the 1992 nomination, as had another Southern governor sixteen years before. Then, in the largest election turnout ever, more than 100 million voters produced the most sweeping Democratic presidential victory since Lyndon Johnson. Nearly 80 percent of registered voters got to the polls, 55 percent of the voting-age population. Bill clinton's 69 percent of the electoral vote gave him a 370-168 win.

Pollsters routinely missed the mark during the campaign when analyzing where evangelicals stood. They guessed the evangelical vote would split fairly evenly between Bush and Southern Baptist Clinton. They were wrong. According to *New York Times* exit polls, 61 percent of white, born-again voters supported Bush, 23 percent supported Clinton, and 15 percent supported independent Ross Perot. Voter Research & Surveys, a cooperative project of major media outlets, reported that 28 percent of Bush's voters were white evangelicals, compared to 14 percent of Perot's and 9 percent of Clinton's.

Once again evangelicals were a factor. When George Bush seemed to weaken on some traditional values issues and generally failed to convince Americans that he deserved a second term, his 1988 evangelical support dropped 20 percent, with Perot capturing 15 of that and Clinton picking up 5.

SENATE ELECTIONS

It is tempting to write concerning a number of classic, close Senate contests, like New Hampshire's in 1974 with its two-vote margin—on the second recount. Here's another, the 1984 Republican Senate primary in Texas. The actual vote totals of the three candidates were 455,768, 454,807, and 454,497. Former

Democratic Rep. Kent Hance topped the Republican list with his 33.4 percent plurality. A few more friends helping, a few more contributions, and either of the finishers with 33.3 percent each could have grabbed the top spot. Unfortunately for Hance, he lost the run-off a few weeks later. I was watching that race because, at the time, Hance and I were members of the same church in suburban Virginia.

The biggest Senate election story in a quarter century developed in 1980. The election of Ronald Reagan combined with the totally unexpected turnover in the U.S. Senate recorded 7.8 on the Richter Scale of Washington's political seismograph. Going into election day, the Senate remained controlled by the Democrats, as it had been for twenty-six consecutive years. They had fifty-nine seats[3] to the Republicans' forty-one. After the votes were tallied that night, twelve seats shifted, every one from the Democratic into the Republican column.

Republicans were ecstatic. To the victors go the spoils. Thanks to their 53-47, they would now chair all committees and appoint two-thirds of the committee staffs. They would be able to assist President Reagan to jam on government's brakes, make a hard right turn, if not a U-turn, and start cutting back on both government spending and federal taxation. A remarkable new day had dawned in U.S. politics.

Equally remarkable were the margins that made possible this major upset. Eleven Senate elections were won with 51 percent or less of the vote, and only two of those were Democrat wins, Hart (CO) and Leahy (VT). Nine of the closest elections went to Republicans, plus D'Amato's (NY) 45-44 percent in a three-way race. Barely squeaking through with 50 percent were Goldwater (AZ), Symms (ID), and East (NC). At 51 percent were Denton (AL), Hawkins (FL), Mattingly (GA), Specter

(PA), and Kasten (WI). Two more Republican victories were achieved with 52 percent of the vote.

The moral of this story? If they had only known, volunteers being the key to victory, the Democrats would surely have put enough troops into several of those very close contests to foil the Republican takeover. But they didn't. On such margins history hangs.

Republicans kept control of the Senate in 1982, but barely. Of thirty-four Senate races, fourteen saw winners with 52 percent or less of the vote. Looking at the numbers, I calculated that a shift of less than 35,000 votes in Missouri, Nevada, Rhode Island, Vermont, and Wyoming, could have given Democrats those five seats, allowing them to wrest control from the GOP. That didn't happen either.

The tables were turned in 1986, when Democrats regained control of the Senate in the middle of Ronald Reagan's second term. That marked the death-knell of his effectiveness with Congress. This time the seven closest elections were all won by Democrats. Senator Conrad won with 50 percent. Senators Shelby (AL), Cranston (CA), Wirth (CO), Fowler (GA), Reid (NV), and Adams (WA) all topped out with 51 percent. Now Republicans had the unpleasant task of second-guessing themselves and asking, "What if…?"

Eight years later, in the watershed 1994 elections, the GOP regained control of the Senate by a 53-47 majority. None of the elections were close, and for the first time in modern politics, the entire freshman class was of one party. Eight of the eleven new GOP senators could be counted on to support a pro-family, traditional values agenda. With a gain of five, a pro-life majority of at least 45-38 was achieved, remaining senators voting mixed records.

This might be a good time to answer a question thoughtful evangelicals often ask: Is it possible for a genuinely Christian candidate to win in the political major leagues? Without hesitation, the answer is yes. There are many examples in Congress, but consider Senator William L. Armstrong's 1984 campaign in Colorado. The senator had sponsored the congressional resolution making 1983 The Year of the Bible, and television spots were then being shown in his state which asked, "Is being a U.S. Senator the most important thing in Bill Armstrong's life? No. His relationship with God is." Viewers were invited to send for a book about their relationship with God.

Political advisors urged Armstrong to pull the spots from the air, but this NAE "Layman of the Year" said no. He insisted on doing what he believed God wanted, and letting the chips fall where they might. His opponent, Lieutenant Governor Nancy Dick, charged, "This man wants to force his beliefs down your throat," and those beliefs, she hastened to add, included a pro-life position as well as his personal faith. In spite of that, Armstrong even led President Reagan in Colorado and was reelected with 64 percent of the vote. Accuser Nancy Dick's 36 percent was the lowest percentage ever for a Democrat in a Colorado Senate race.

But what about today? That was 1984. Ten years later, two other NAE "Laymen of the Year" had won seats in the upper chamber: returning Sen. Dan Coats of Indiana and incoming Sen. John Ashcroft of Missouri. Committed Christians can win in the political major leagues.

HOUSE ELECTIONS

Wisecracks about Congress are common. What is uncommon is a willingness on the part of critics to work to alter the

435 member House of Representatives. Obviously, change must come one congressional district at a time. Evangelicals must take responsibility for the district in which they live.

Since 1966, except for the Watergate year of 1974, House elections have seen over 90 percent of members seeking reelection. Political recidivism has been on the increase. In 1986, 383 of 395 representatives running for another term were successful—an impressive 97 percent rate of return. Still, forty seats were being vacated so 10 percent of House elections would automatically put new faces into Congress. In 1988, the House success rate for incumbents fighting to keep their seats was over 98 percent.

Such statistics at first blush are terribly discouraging to challengers and to those thinking of joining their campaigns. On the other hand, after the 1988 elections I discovered to my amazement that 63 percent of all current representatives had entered Congress in the eighties. There is a significant turnover during every election cycle, whether of members leaving to run for other offices (usually the Senate or governor), retiring, or dying.

As public cynicism has grown concerning Congress, the rate of change has picked up dramatically. After the 1992 elections, there were 110 new faces in the House, and 1994's elections added another eighty-six. Although a number of 1992 winners were defeated in 1994, still a significant percentage of the members of the House of Representatives are now serving in their first or second term. Challengers' chances for winning a seat in Congress have greatly increased, and the current public call for term limits will accelerate the momentum.

There is never a shortage of close House elections. Take 1984. In Idaho, a Democratic challenger unseated the incumbent by 67 votes out of 202,000. A Republican captured an open seat in Utah by just 143 of 209,000 votes. In Pennsylvania, an incumbent successfully defended his seat by 481 of 248,000 votes. And it took until April to determine that Rep. Frank McCloskey had held onto his Indiana seat by a razor-thin four votes out of 233,000.

Look at 1986. Three Republican incumbents very narrowly won their battles to stay in Congress: by 81 out of 145,000 in North Carolina; 166 out of 152,000 in Indiana; and 211 out of 188,000 in Minnesota. Former NBA basketball player Tom McMillen (D) Maryland won an open seat by 510 out of 129,000, incidentally becoming the tallest member of Congress. Are you wondering about the significantly lower district vote totals in 1986 compared to 1984? Voters participate in much higher numbers in a presidential election year, and 1986 was not such a year.

Compare the next several elections. In 1988 Washington and Oregon incumbents won by 618 and 707 votes out of about 220,000, and a Florida challenger unseated a senior Democrat by 732 votes out of 250,000. In 1990, a Missouri congressman lost his seat by just 54 votes of 188,207. In 1992, one Democrat and one Republican captured their seats by fewer than 600 votes each.

In 1994, after forty years in the minority, Republicans gained fifty-two House seats to become the majority by 230-205. In the process, not only was no Republican seeking reelection to Senate, House, or a governor's mansion defeated, but no pro-life incumbent was defeated by a pro-choice challenger. Now even the National Abortion Rights Action League (NARAL) admits there are 218 anti-abortion votes in the House, including six newly elected women. Reliable abortion supporters number 146 and the remaining seventy-one sometimes vote pro-life and sometimes pro-choice. Conversely, twenty-four pro-life challengers defeated pro-abortion incumbents for House seats.

That year, an incumbent from Connecticut kept his seat by only four votes. One Republican who thought she had won by ninety-three had the result overturned on a recount. Four other races had margins ranging from 200 to 550 votes. But here's the kind of thing political strategists note. One-third of House Democrats had marginal victories of 55 percent or less, making them vulnerable in 1996, while just 5 percent of Republicans were in that category.

Polls often reveal which races will be highly competitive, but they do not accurately reveal where the narrowest of margins will be found. Wise evangelicals must therefore become part of the campaigns of appreciated incumbents or admirable challengers. The conventional wisdom, by the way, is that challengers should always be willing to run at least twice. Gains in experience, name recognition, and organizational effectiveness could put your candidate in Congress the second time around, if not the first.

In the mid-1990s, congressional districts average 600,000 citizens. Madison Project statistics say that while 70 percent of those, or 415,000 are eligible to vote, just 290,000 of them will register, and that amounts to only 48 percent of the total population. Of those, only 27 percent or 160,000 will actually vote, so that ultimately as few as 13.51 percent of the total, 80,001 citizens, will decide who wins. Not bad. From 600,000 to only 80,000 plus one. The votes you produce for your candidate count more than you may have realized.

REDISTRICTING AND GERRYMANDERING

Amateur political strategists need to be reminded of another critical feature on the political landscape, pivotal for the makeup of the House. After each decade's official U.S. census, congressional districts around the nation are reapportioned so that the various states get their share according to population. The idea is that the districts be as nearly equal in population as possible. Once it became known, for example, that California's House delegation would grow from forty-five to fifty-two in 1991, several new district boundary plans were designed.

State government controls the redrawing process. Where one party has the governor and a majority in both houses of the legislature, the likelihood that these lines will be gerrymandered to that party's advantage are, conservatively, 100 percent. The time-honored practice of gerrymandering, which ignores natural geographical boundaries in favor of political considerations, comes from Elbridge Gerry, a signer of the Declaration of Independence and governor of Massachusetts. When a district drawn to his instructions looked like a salamander, some wit combined Gerry's name with the salamander's to dub the new creature the Gerrymander.

The redistricting process in fifty states explains why, after the 1992 election, the percentage of Democrats and Republicans in the House differed considerably from the total vote. Nationwide, Democrats won 43.7 million congressional votes while Republicans trailed with 37.2 million. That's 54 percent to 46 percent. Yet the Democrats, with 258 members to the Republicans' 176, held a 59 to 40.5 lead in House seats.

California shows what flagrant gerrymandering can do. In 1984, 4,228,000 congressional ballots were cast for Republicans across the state, to 4,210,000 for Democrats. Nevertheless, Democrats sent twenty-seven Representatives to the House while the GOP sent a meager eighteen. Democrats controlled 60 percent of the House seats with only 49.9 percent of the popular vote. Their 27-18 edge had not changed by the end of the decade.

Now you know why the national party committees invest as heavily as they do in their state organizations. The party that loses the bulk of the redistricting struggles will be behind the eightball in Congress for a decade to come. Astute evangelicals will see the folly of ignoring state level politics to focus only on national.

RACES THAT ENDED IN A TIE

The all-time close election among state legislatures came in 1978, when the Pennsylvania House of Representatives found each party controlling 101 seats, with the remaining seat deadlocked at 8,551 votes. It took a recount to break the tie and award the seat—by fourteen votes. You never know.

Here's another implausible victory. Illinois State Rep. Penny Pullen apparently lost by thirty-one votes in her 1990 primary battle against a one-issue, pro-abortion challenger funded by the National Abortion Rights Action League. An evangelical, Penny was an acknowledged leader of the pro-life forces in Illinois. When a recount produced an exact tie, a state-sponsored coin flip awarded the seat to her opponent, but Pullen took the matter to the Illinois Supreme Court, arguing that the intent of some of the previously rejected ballots could be determined. Discovering that eight of the thirty ballots had partial holes in the punch card ballots, the court gave her opponent just one of those and Penny seven—and the nomination. Dozens of Penny's friends flocked around her afterward and chorused, "If we had only known it would be so close, we would have rushed to help you."

A PRESIDENT AND A WOULD-BE PRESIDENT

Comparatively unimportant elections here or there can trigger events that channel the flow of history. Lyndon Johnson "won" his first primary election for the U.S. Senate in 1948, by eighty-seven votes out of more than 988,000 cast. It now is evident that Johnson raised the art of campaign fraud to new heights that year, as he demonstrably stole the election.[4] By a mere eighty-seven vote margin, by fair means and foul, LBJ put himself into position one day to be president. Never a senator, never a president. Once in the Oval Office, Johnson would fail to conclude the war in Vietnam but succeed in passing the massive spending programs of his "Great Society"—programs creating entitlements that have much to do with today's budget deficits and huge national debt.

In 1962, George S. McGovern was elected to the U.S. Senate from South Dakota by a margin of less than one vote per precinct. Like Johnson, never a senator, never a presidential nominee. In 1972, the liberal McGovern became the Democrats' choice to run against Richard Nixon. As it turned out, McGovern was far too liberal for the American people and Nixon trounced him. Now just suppose that the Democrats had nominated a more moderate candidate that year and that Nixon had been returned to private life. Then the nation would not have been dragged through the anguish of Watergate or forced to witness the resignation of her president. But history worked out another way—hinging on a narrow Senate victory ten years before in the relatively obscure state of South Dakota.

Voters determined the political fortunes of Johnson, McGovern, and all the others in this chapter. But never forget that it was the campaign volunteers who persuaded them how to vote and who, through such narrow victories, literally shaped history. Next time, you must get involved.

WHAT

THE

DEADLINE

DEMANDS

ARE WE "ONE NATION UNDER GOD"?

Although no question mark will be found in his magnificent speech, still, Abraham Lincoln expressed a disquieting uncertainty in his Gettysburg Address: "…whether that nation or any nation so conceived and so dedicated can long endure." While his immediate concern was the Civil War, his implicit question is as relevant today as it was in 1863. The United States of America, as a nation, has no guarantee of perpetuity.

God Almighty, the maker of heaven and earth, "will judge the world in righteousness" (Psalm 96:13, 98:9). The God before whom "the nations are like a drop in a bucket…as dust on the scales" (Isaiah 40:15) will "judge all the nations on every side" (Joel 3:12). A cursory look at the Old Testament will reveal how the Lord of the nations judges nations within history. Even with Israel, there is a cycle: rebellion, retribution, repentance, restoration.

Those who understand and believe biblical teaching know full well that the God who "sets up kings and deposes them" (Daniel 2:21) may one day call down judgment upon our nation. Our national security and longevity are ultimately under his control. For that reason, it is critical to ask: Are we "one nation under God"—as we say we are when we pledge allegiance to the flag?

The average American is far too ignorant of his spiritual heritage, but the fault may lie with others. Textbook writers have cut from the pages of history facts considered too controversial or unappealing to the educational elite who prefer books sanitized of religious references for America's classrooms.

As mentioned in Chapter 4, again consider the first half of the Mayflower Compact of 1620, as printed in the Teacher's Guide for the high school history text *Triumph of the American Nation*, published by Harcourt Brace Jovanovich in 1986: "We whose names are underwritten, having undertaken a voyage to plant the first colony in the northern parts of Virginia, do solemnly and in the presence of one another, covenant and combine ourselves together into a civil body politic..."[1]

Blown off course by storms and arriving in Massachusetts, where their landing is today marked by Plymouth Rock, the Pilgrims came with a much deeper purpose that is hidden by the preceding deceptive account, which deletes almost every reference to God. Here, in contrast, is the actual opening of the Mayflower Compact, all words restored (although not in olde English spelling):

> In the name of God, Amen. We whose names are underwritten, the loyal subjects of our dread sovereign lord, King James, by the grace of God, of Great Britain, France, and Ireland, King, Defender of the Faith, etc., having undertaken for the glory of God and advance-

ment of the Christian faith and honor of our king and country, a voyage to plant the first colony in the northern parts of Virginia, do by these presents solemnly and in the presence of God, and one of another, covenant and combine ourselves together into a civil body politic..."

The *vision realized* by our Founding Fathers—that of "one nation under God"—was a *vision revised* in the mid-twentieth century, and today or tomorrow may well be a *vision revived.*

THE VISION REALIZED

The new nation was conceived with the adoption of the Declaration of Independence on July 4, 1776. The fledgling nation in turn was born with the ratification of the Constitution on September 17, 1787. These dates mark the period when our Founding Fathers realized their vision.

In Deuteronomy, Moses reminded Israel of four historic realities regarding their national relationship to God. The historical record (unaltered version) demonstrates that America's Founding Fathers believed that those same realities applied to their new nation. I do not suggest there is an exact parallel here. The United States of America is no contemporary equivalent of Israel, God's chosen Old Testament people and, in the judgment of most evangelicals, Israel remains a people with whom God still has a special covenant relationship. But there is a biblical passage that assuredly does apply to the United States. A universal spiritual principle, it is apropos to any nation or individual: "From everyone who has been given much, much will be demanded; and from the one who has been entrusted with much, much more will be asked" (Luke 12:48).

Here are the historic realities of God's dealing with Israel as a nation:

• Their *Preservation by God* (Deuteronomy 8:1-5,14b-16). This had been an enslaved people, led out of oppression and through a terrible wilderness, preserved through miraculous events. While Moses was their leader, he humbly acknowledged that God brought them out.

• The *Providence of God* (Deuteronomy 8:7-9). They would not find their new land through scouting and exploring skills or by chance, but God would bring them to it by his own hand. The land would have an adequate water supply, a good growing climate, and mineral wealth for making agricultural implements.

• Their *Prosperity from God* (Deuteronomy 8:10-13,18). They would eat well, have time to settle in and build fine homes, and see their flocks and herds reproduce. The land would even include silver and gold for trading and later a monetary system. Beyond all that, God would give them the ability to produce wealth.

• The *Punishment of God* (Deuteronomy 8:1,6,11,17-20). This reality would always be on the horizon, perhaps only as foreboding as a cloud the size of a man's hand, but always there. The people of Israel are clearly told that if they do not honor God, if they flout his will by ignoring or violating his commands, laws, and decrees, then they will be destroyed as a nation.

Now we turn from Israel's sacred text to America's most venerable document, the Declaration of Independence. It is no mere coincidence that the four historic realities recognized by Moses are reflected in the Declaration.

• Their *Preservation by God.*

> When in the Course of human events, it becomes necessary for one people to dissolve the political bands which have connected them with another, and to assume among the Powers of the earth, the separate and equal station to which the Laws of Nature and of Nature's God entitle them, a decent respect to the opinions of mankind requires that they should declare the causes which impel them to the separation....

> The history of the present King of Great Britain is a history of repeated injuries and usurpations, all having in direct object the establishment of an absolute Tyranny over these States. To prove this, let Facts be submitted to a candid world....

Then follows the major body of the Declaration, a list of charges against the king, but the major thrust of these words is that, like Israel, Americans had suffered injustice and tyranny from which they had been preserved. Both natural law and the laws of God in Scripture entitled them to exist separately. As Israel came out of Egypt, our forefathers came out of Europe. Their "wilderness" was a dangerous Atlantic Ocean.

• The *Providence of God.*
"And for the support of this Declaration, with a firm reliance

on the Protection of Divine Providence, we mutually pledge to each other our Lives, our Fortunes, and our sacred Honor."

No explanatory comment is needed about this final sentence of the Declaration, which uses the very theological word in question.

- Their *Prosperity from God.*

> We hold these truths to be self-evident, that all men are created equal, that they are endowed by their Creator with certain unalienable Rights, that among these are Life, Liberty and the pursuit of Happiness. That to secure these rights, Governments are instituted among Men, deriving their just powers from the consent of the governed... .

The Founding Fathers knew that it would be foolhardy and impossible for government, in and of itself, to attempt to provide happiness. However, citizens of this free land would have the right to pursue happiness because of their prior rights to life and liberty—all of which were God-given. That being the case, no government could legitimately claim to grant such rights, but only to guarantee or secure them. Thus, citizens achieving prosperity should thank God for it.

- The *Punishment of God.*

"We, therefore, the Representatives of the United States of America, in General Congress, Assembled, appealing to the Supreme Judge of the world for the rectitude of our intentions, do, in the Name, and by authority of the good People of these Colonies, solemnly publish and declare, That these United

Colonies are, and of Right ought to be Free and Independent States..."

As they separated from the English crown, our forebearers called upon God to examine the integrity of their motivation. They tacitly acknowledged that if their intentions were not righteous, they could not expect God's blessing upon their new venture. It is well-nigh impossible to envision a piece of legislation coming from Congress in the 1990s with a respectful call for God to evaluate it. In those days, such words were not surprising.

Can anyone doubt that the authors and signers of the Declaration by common consent acknowledged their political creation to be "one nation under God"? For anyone skeptical of these biblical convictions of the Founding Fathers, anyone suspicious that the author cleverly contrived this parallel in his own mind, consider the words of Thomas Jefferson. Our third president proposed a national seal portraying Moses leading the chosen people into the promised land and, in his second inaugural address in 1805, Jefferson was specific: "I shall need, too, the favor of that Being in whose hands we are, who led our fathers, as Israel of old, from their native land and planted them in a country flowing with all the necessaries and comforts of life; who has covered our infancy with His providence and our riper years with His wisdom and power..."

Rep. Guy VanderJagt (R-MI), at the National Prayer Breakfast in February 1980, without any fear of contradiction stated: "Our Declaration of Independence is first of all a declaration of dependence on God." The Founding Fathers would have stood with him. After six months as president, George Washington issued a Proclamation for a National Thanksgiving, including these expressions:

Whereas it is the duty of all nations to acknowledge the providence of Almighty God, to obey
His will, to be grateful for His benefits, and
humbly to implore His protection and favor....
And also that we may then unite in most
humbly offering our prayers and supplications
to the great Lord and Ruler of Nations, and
beseech Him to pardon our national and other
transgressions...[2]

Hear part of Washington's first inaugural address:

...No people can be bound to acknowledge
and adore the Invisible Hand which conducts
the affairs of men more than those of the
United States.... We ought to be no less persuaded that the propitious smiles of Heaven
can never be expected on a nation that disre-
gards the eternal rules of order and right which
Heaven itself has ordained...[3]

Recall Washington's farewell address:

Of all the dispositions and habits which lead to
political prosperity, Religion and Morality are
indispensable supports.... Where is the security
for property, for reputation, for life, if the sense
of religious obligation deserts the oaths which
are the instrument of investigation in Courts of
Justice? And let us with caution indulge in the
supposition that morality can be maintained
without religion. Whatever may be conceded to

the influence of refined education on minds of peculiar structure, reason and experience both forbid us to expect that national morality can prevail in exclusion of religious principle...[4]

John Adams would become our first vice president and then succeed Washington as our second president. As independence neared, he wrote to his wife Abigail in 1775: "It is Religion and Morality alone which can establish the principles upon which freedom can securely stand. A patriot must be a religious man."[5]

Not long after Washington's inauguration, Adams wrote:

We have no government armed with power capable of contending with human passions unbridled by morality and religion. Avarice, ambition, revenge, or gallantry, would break the strongest cords of our Constitution as a whale goes through a net.... Our Constitution was made only for a moral and religious people. It is wholly inadequate to the government of any other.[6]

Speaking to the first meeting of Congress in Washington, in the original Capitol in 1800, Adams said:

It would be unbecoming the Representatives of this nation to assemble, for the first time, in this solemn temple, without looking up to the Supreme Ruler of the Universe, and imploring his blessing. Here, and throughout our country, may simple manners, pure morals, and true religion, flourish forever![7]

Thomas Jefferson, before becoming our third president, in 1781 asked: "Can the liberties of a nation be thought secure when we have removed their only firm basis, a conviction in the minds of the people that these liberties are the gift of God?"[8]

Critics of attempts to demonstrate the biblical beliefs of our Founding Fathers sometimes dismiss them with a wave: "They weren't really Christians, just a bunch of deists." Through meticulous documentation, John Eidsmoe has demolished the myth that these were mostly secular men in his book, *Christianity and the Constitution—The Faith of Our Founding Fathers*. Reading his in-depth studies of thirteen major founders of our nation, I conclude that in today's terminology eight should be called evangelicals, three would be termed Christians in a broader sense, and only two were deists, Jefferson and Benjamin Franklin. The latter two moved closer to historic Christianity in later years, and some Christian beliefs (of which they might not have been conscious) colored their speech and writings.

Deism is sub-Christian in its "clockmaker" view of the universe, namely, that God created it like a clock already wound up, and then left the world to run down on its own. With that in mind, Jefferson was, at best, an inconsistent deist. His own words, inscribed on the wall of the Jefferson Memorial, bear witness that he believed in a God of justice who acts in history: "Indeed I tremble for my country when I reflect that God is just: that his justice cannot sleep for ever…"

The author of the Bill of Rights, including the First Amendment with its religion clauses, became our fourth president. This was James Madison's conviction: "Before any man can be considered as a member of Civil Society, he must be considered as a subject of the Governor of the Universe."[9]

Except for four vice presidents who came into office on the death of a president and who therefore made no formal inaugural remarks,[10] every president of the United States has sought divine help in his inaugural speech. The tendency today is to downplay such words as a formality, but the kind of strong sentiments uttered by the first four presidents have been sincerely echoed by our most recent conservative presidents, Ronald Reagan and George Bush, by our current liberal president, Bill Clinton, and by other twentieth-century presidents of differing ideologies. Note the words of two of them:

> The fundamental basis of this nation's law was given to Moses on the Mount. The fundamental basis of our Bill of Rights comes from the teachings which we get from Exodus and St. Matthew, from Isaiah and St. Paul. I don't think we emphasize that enough these days. If we don't have the proper fundamental moral background, we will finally wind up with a totalitarian government which does not believe in rights for anybody except the state.

> No greater thing could come to our land today than a revival of the spirit of religion—a revival that would sweep through the homes of the nation and stir the hearts of men and women of all faiths to a reassertion of their belief in God and their dedication to His will for themselves and their world. I doubt if there is any problem—social, political or economic —that would not melt away before the fire of such a spiritual awakening.[11]

The first may sound like a quotation from 1988 presidential contender Pat Robertson, but the words were Harry Truman's. The second may resemble comments by Ronald Reagan, but it was Franklin Roosevelt who spoke them.

America's Founding Fathers did not form a Christian State, but they clearly established their new nation on Judeo-Christian principles found in the Bible.[12] Just at this point, I almost expect someone to come forward with a triumphant flourish in an attempt to destroy my case, charging that God is not even mentioned in the Constitution.

One is tempted to ask, with a sardonic smile, whether the challengers have read the Constitution. After Article VII, I find: "Done in Convention by the Unanimous Consent of the States present the Seventeenth Day of December in the Year of our Lord one thousand seven hundred and eighty seven..."

To be technical, the name of God is there after all. Let's be fair, however. That was the standard way of signing official documents in those days. Other than that, God is not mentioned in a substantive way. But no matter. Such an argument is misplaced because it overlooks the Constitution's basis on our foundational document, the Declaration of Independence.

The Declaration is our national articles of incorporation, and the Constitution is a set of bylaws under which we govern ourselves. The Declaration and the Constitution cannot be separated from one another.

THE VISION REVISED

A 1947 decision appeared to provide the Supreme Court an opportunity to "baptize" into the Constitution a phrase that had never been there—and in so doing, to revise our forefathers' vision of "one nation under God." It is not necessary to know the details of *Everson v. Board of Education*, but rather to learn that, in *Everson*, the court for the first time said that the Non-establishment clause of the First Amendment "was intended to erect 'a wall of separation between church and state.'" Enlarging on the concept, Justice Black wrote: "That wall must be kept high and impregnable."

Everson became the pivotal case for establishment issues, for four decades influencing the court's decisions in a direction not in accord with historic facts. While the pendulum has begun to swing back in recent years, the interpretation and imagery of a high and impregnable wall of separation has guided the court toward secularizing the United States, in the process often creating an impression of hostility toward religion.

Seven years later, however, Congress appeared to challenge this view of separation when it added to the words of the pledge of allegiance the phrase "under God." What possible secular purpose could that 1954 action have had? Congress compounded its challenge when it ordered the inscription "In God We Trust" to be placed on our money in 1955, and when it made the phrase our national motto in 1956—an admission that the state is not sovereign unto itself, but accountable to a higher authority.

Was court or Congress correct? The historical documents and facts do not lead to the conclusion that the framers of the First Amendment and the Congress responsible for its adoption into the Constitution intended a wall of absolute separation between church and state. However, and this is a critical point, there are those who contend that what the framers intended is oftentimes impossible to determine, and in any case not binding for today. Some of them are Supreme Court justices.

The 1983 case of *Marsh v. Chambers* illustrates the issue. The High Court considered the constitutionality of Nebraska's paying a minister to serve as chaplain to its legislature, to open each session with prayer. Happily, by a six to three vote the Court approved the practice. In the majority opinion, Chief Justice Burger pointed out that the first Congress authorized the appointment of paid chaplains for both the Senate and House just three days before it reached final agreement on the language of the Bill of Rights. "Clearly the men who wrote the First Amendment Religion Clause did not view paid legislative chaplains and opening prayers as a violation of that Amendment," he wrote. Incidentally, James Madison, author of the First Amendment, served on the congressional committee of six that recommended the chaplain system.

As important as was the affirmation in *Marsh*, the three dissenting votes are extremely significant. In this case, all the justices had been made aware of the historical sequence above, so that it was not necessary to engage in conjecture about the intent of the Founders. Nonetheless, three justices were willing to say, in effect, that paid chaplains in state legislatures should be held unconstitutional. To them, what the Framers intended was beside the point. They were willing to substitute their personal preference for a strict interpretation of the Constitution—an act of judicial activism.

Renowned constitutional attorney William Bentley Ball candidly condemns the activist approach by which judges seek to correct what they see as abuses in the system, but which legislative bodies have failed to remedy. Said Ball: "The Constitution must govern our judges, and not the reverse." Judges who share that attitude bring judicial restraint to the bench, seeing their job only as interpreting and applying the Constitution. Think of the consequences if the Supreme Court should have a majority of activists. Unanchored as they would be, five non-elected justices, serving for life, could create a sociological revolution in American society. Some strongly argue that the Court already has.

To grasp once and for all the importance of judicial philosophy, think of an analogy: What the Bible is to Christianity, the Constitution is to the United States—in both cases the absolute, final, written authority. If you take a liberal view of the Bible, by which the words are not necessarily binding and the intent of the author is irrelevant, then the form of Christianity that you develop may bear little resemblance to the intent of the Founding Father in heaven. By the same token, if you take a liberal view of the Constitution, the nation that you shape may not resemble the intent of America's Founding Fathers. In that light, anyone can see how it has been possible for the Court to revise the Founders' original vision for our nation. Further, we remind ourselves again of the extreme importance of selecting presidents because they appoint judges.

One loose end remains. Where did the "wall of separation" concept originate, and how did it play out in the originator's life? In 1802, President Thomas Jefferson interpreted his understanding of the First Amendment to the Danbury Baptist Association of Connecticut. He was writing eleven years after the First Amendment was approved, and not as a jurist. While he probably was not suggesting that religion be walled off, his terminology caught on and came to be accepted as what the Constitution implied.

Now for the second part of the question. How did Jefferson apply his own concept of the "wall"? In 1803, a year after the Danbury letter, President Jefferson made a treaty with the Kaskaskia Indians in which he pledged federal money to support their priest and to build them a Catholic church.[13] Later that year he sought funds from Congress to finance the obligations of the treaty. It is more than mildly astounding that the author of the "wall of separation" concept asked Congress to fund religious activity in his own time. It is, therefore, unthinkable that Jefferson would have allowed his country to be stripped of religiously-based values so that it could no longer be considered "under God."

THE VISION REVIVED

In the opinion of some thoughtful political analysts, a movement to revive the "one nation under God" vision of the Founding Fathers began to develop in the last decade. "Forget nuclear freezes and yuppies," wrote *New Republic* senior editor Fred Barnes. "The most important political development of the '80s is the emergence of the evangelical voting bloc."[14]

Millions of evangelicals might not have been able to analyze the reasons for their unprecedented involvement in politics, but they were responding either to the calls of respected Christian leaders or to a growing uneasiness in their own minds. Revision of the nation's moral codes was being aided and abetted by the courts and the Congress. Government agencies seemed to be getting their noses under the tent of the churches' religious liberty.

Moreover, the bottom line for evangelicals' burgeoning political interest is the conviction that God's commands are for our good (Deuteronomy 4:40, 5:33, 6:3). Individually, those who violate God's laws are sure to be hurt. That is true in both spiritual and physical realms.

Nationally, when a country flouts God's moral and spiritual principles, it is in for tough times. One Old Testament chapter devotes sixty-eight verses to the blessings of national obedience and the curses of national disobedience of God's laws (Deuteronomy 28).

Even if some of their fellow citizens do not appreciate it, evangelicals are now self-consciously serving their culture by devoting themselves to political values consistent with their understanding of biblical values. They are eager to see their nation willingly acknowledge itself to be "one nation under God." Having read some of the Founders' convictions earlier in this chapter, evangelicals will be delighted to find themselves in such distinguished company as the first presidents.

What is more, evangelicals are strengthening our national foundations from a sociological standpoint as well as a spiritual one. In an article on "Democracy and Religion," the Brookings Institution's James Reichley explored the relation between democratic and Judeo-Christian values.[15] He took issue with many of his peers: "The Founders, who included among their number some of the most acute political theorists the nation ever produced did not share the disinterest in religion of more recent generations of political scientists."

Apparently they knew something today's academic establishment has missed. Reichley finds only three secular sources which can be expected to support democratic institutions: social habit, self-interest, and self-sacrifice. He argues that social habit, developed through custom and tradition, will inevitably fail. Since the Enlightenment, Reichley finds social and political thinkers distrusting religion and attempting to construct moral philosophies based on either "the rational pursuit of individual self-interest...[or] submergence of the individual in an idealized general will." The one track has typified democracies, and the other authoritarian socialism or communism.

Reichley can only conclude that Republican government needs the guidance and support of religious principles. Democracy, for its part, depends, now and for the foreseeable future, on values that have no reliable source outside religion.

And those were the rock-solid convictions of our Founding Fathers.

Wil and Ariel Durant, in their monumental *Story of Civilization*, came to similar conclusions. They assert that, without a standard of public morality, no society has ever survived. It is just as clear that no moral standard has survived without religious support.

Evangelicals have more than enough cause to be deeply concerned about Lincoln's haunting question, "whether that nation or any nation so conceived or so dedicated can long endure." If they and many of their fellow Americans cannot revive the vision of the Founders, their nation will be in jeopardy. Given the loss of our moral consensus and the serious deterioration of our culture in the United States today, it is tragically evident that we are no longer "one nation under God." But we could be.

WHO WILL DETERMINE AMERICA'S FUTURE?

Two major stories headlined the front page of the *Fort Lauderdale Sun-Sentinel* on January 23, 1994. At the top was the sickening report of the point-blank shooting of a taxi-driver by three teen-age girls, thirteen, fifteen, and seventeen, who chose to put a bullet in the back of the driver's head rather than pay a $6 cab fare. Below that was a photograph and article about demonstrators outside the Coral Ridge Presbyterian Church, protesting former vice president Dan Quayle's Saturday night address at the church's "Reclaiming America" conference.

Having spoken at that conference, and shocked at the brutal killing, I bought the Sunday paper especially to see how the two events were covered. The *Sun-Sentinel* pooh-poohed Quayle's message and lauded the protesters' picket signs demanding tolerance for any and all kinds of "families," without any moral discrimination. Inside the paper, however, police and youth counselors showed wisdom beyond the editors'. In interviews, they deplored children fending for themselves, all too many of them from single-parent homes where the mother could not possibly know what her kids were doing. A police sergeant lamented that "We have a nation of kids coming up that will devour us. No morals are being taught to our kids." As sociologists well know, such children often find a sense of belonging in gangs, where criminal behavior is acceptable and encouraged.

How can so many Americans stubbornly refuse to admit the obvious? Common sense is disappearing. An important newspaper sees no connection between its trashing the pro-family message of a former vice president of the United States and the tragic consequences of family breakdown. That June, the cabby's seventeen-year-old murderer was found guilty of first-degree murder. Her two younger friends awaited trial, as adults, on the same charge.

At the dedication of Focus on the Family's new Colorado Springs facilities in 1993, former White House special counsel Charles Colson told of his realization, twenty years before, that the Watergate episode that brought down Richard Nixon was at heart a battle for the government of the United States. But today? "Now there is a battle for the soul of America—one that makes Watergate look like child's play."

Several years ago, while writing *Winning the New Civil War*, I read the as yet unpublished manuscript of *Culture Wars*, University of Virginia scholar James Davison Hunter's book. Three years later, Hunter published *Before the Shooting Begins: Searching for Democracy in America's Culture War*. There is a sobering nuance of meaning in his titles. Earlier, he wrote of "culture wars"—skirmishes or battles here and there. Now his title ominously hints at one all-out, all-embracing culture war.

Congressman Henry Hyde (R-IL) helps us define America's "Kulturkampf—a culture war, a war between cultures and a war about the very meaning of 'culture.'"

It is best to be precise about the terminology here. By "culture war," I don't mean arguments over the relative merits of Mozart and Beethoven...Nor do I mean the tensions between highbrows and lowbrows, between sports fans and opera buffs, between people who think Bruce Springsteen is the greatest artist alive and people who wouldn't know Bruce Springsteen if he rang their doorbell and asked to use the telephone.

No, by "culture war" I mean the struggle between those who believe that the norms of "bourgeois morality"...should form the ethical basis of our common life, and those who are determined that those norms will be replaced with a radical and thoroughgoing moral relativism.[1]

Having lived in exile in the United States, but at last returned to his beloved Russia, one of the most courageous and perceptive men of our century thinks that the wrong forces are winning those wars. In a *Time* interview, Alexander Solzhenitsyn hit the nail on the head when he responded to a question about the decline of the moral life of the West:

There is technical progress, but this is not the same thing as the progress of humanity as such. In every civilization this process is very complex. In Western civilizations—which used to be called Western-Christian but now might better be called Western-Pagan—along with the development of intellectual life and science, there has been a loss of the serious moral basis of society.[2]

Once again, the word *culture* for our purposes here does not mean preferences, tastes, and manners. What is culture?

It is the ways of thinking, living and behaving that define a people and underlie its achievements. It is a nation's collective mind, its sense of right and wrong, the way it perceives reality, and its definition of self. Culture is the morals and habits a mother strives to instill in her children. It is the obligations we acknowledge toward our neighbors, our community, and our government.... It is the standards we set and enforce for ourselves and for others: our definitions of duty, honor, and character. It is our collective conscience.[3]

By that or any other realistic definition of culture, it has become obvious that our nation is sliding down a slippery slope toward decadence, gathering speed as it goes. Evangelicals who do not have their heads in the sand will agree. But will they now seize the opportunity to steer America's course, something I believe to be within their grasp? That remains to be seen.

COMPETING FORCES IN THE CULTURE WAR

Because ideas have consequences, we must understand the two divergent philosophies that nourish this civil war within our culture. Reduced to bare bones, the battle is between cultural conservatives and cultural radicals. The conservative philosophy ascribes great value to the accumulated wisdom of the culture, and considers disciplined behavior most likely to bring happiness in the long run. The radical philosophy praises novelty, diversity, and experimentation, and tends to find its satisfaction in immediate gratification.

The Founding Fathers assuredly would have taken sides with cultural conservatism, for they often insisted that Christianity and government must work together "to raise the virtue and morality of the people to a level at which they are sufficiently public-spirited and self-restrained that republican government can work."[4]

This distinction becomes even more pointed when one realizes that the ethical standard of Western civilization was the Bible. Cultural radicals are often in direct rebellion against those Judeo-Christian values, unwilling to discipline themselves by any standard beyond themselves. The Founders made social compacts or covenants with each other, God being their witness, and those commitments were a sufficient glue to hold their nation together. By contrast, cultural radicals abhor moral limitations, that is, religiously based values, and exalt the quest for individual rights as their greatest good. However, 250 million people pursuing their own rights will never produce the glue that can hold their society together.

In a speech addressed to a small group of political strategists, conservative political thinker Paul Weyrich developed the case for cultural conservatism:

> Democracy is the one form of government which depends for its success and existence upon a virtuous people. Democracy works only

so long as a sufficient proportion of the people are willing to place the common good above self-interest, and only so long as there is a broad consensus on what constitutes virtue.[5]

Once again, Alexander Solzhenitsyn touches the sore spot of excessive individualism:

...we have two lungs. You can't breathe with just one lung and not with the other. We must avail ourselves of rights and duties in equal measure. And if this is not established by the law, if the law does not oblige us to do that, then we have to control ourselves. When Western society was established, it was based on the idea that each individual limited his own behavior. Everyone understood what he could do and what he could not do. The law itself did not restrain people. Since then, the only thing we have been developing is rights, rights, rights, at the expense of duty.[6]

DESTRUCTIVE EDUCATION

America's younger generation is conditioned toward cultural radicalism today by public education. Allan Bloom's book, *The Closing of the American Mind*, to widespread astonishment, established itself on national best-seller lists in mid-1987. Bloom, himself, had expected to sell only five thousand copies. Neither a fluke nor a public relations triumph, the book's success was a resounding testimony to the force of Bloom's message. The

University of Chicago professor attacked liberalism for selling collegians a bill of goods, namely, that there is no standard for distinguishing between right and wrong, or good and bad. Bruce Shelley summarizes Bloom's thrust:

> ...today's university student believes one thing deeply. It has reached the status of an axiom. He is absolutely convinced that truth is relative, and he is astonished if anyone is foolish enough to challenge the point.

> This relativism is not the product of theoretical reasoning. It is, so the student believes, a moral postulate of a free society. He has been taught from childhood that the danger of absolutism is not error but intolerance. Thus in our democratic society, says Bloom, openness is the highest virtue...the supreme insight is not to think you are right at all.[7]

The darker side of this coin of tolerance is the academic elite's repudiation of the conclusions of "true believers" of any sort—especially evangelicals who believe that God has spoken in sentences they can understand and must obey.

No wonder evangelicals are called narrow-minded, religious zealots, bigoted fundamentalists, censors, or anti-choice activists—and all of that just for failing to smile benignly upon promiscuity, drugs, euthanasia, homosexual lifestyles, or taking the life of an unborn child for convenience—and at the same time trying to get government not to condone such practices.

Popular campus speaker Josh McDowell says that in the

1940s, "the three most common [school] disciplinary problems were talking, chewing gum, and running in the halls. In the 1980s the statistics say the most common problems are rape, robbery, and assault."[8] Our society is paying the price of the sexual revolution, enhanced by values-clarification teaching techniques that undermine the moral instruction of home and church, and exacerbated by teachers who refuse to make moral judgments. A cartoon spoofs this educational craziness under the title, "If drug education were taught like sex education." In the cartoon's four frames, the teacher speaks to the children seated before her:

> I would like to encourage all of you not to use drugs at all. But since this is a public school and I'm not allowed to inflict my own puritan beliefs on you….and since I know that many of you will be active with drugs from time to time, today's class will be on how to practice safe drug use…. This is a hypodermic syringe. You should use this if you want to inject drugs directly into your veins. Notice how it is sealed so the user can tell the needle is clean…. It's important you use clean needles when you inject drugs into your body. If you don't have clean needles, check with the school nurse and she will give you some. Now, let me show you how to find the vein.

Absurd? Agreed. But since many traditional cultural values are no longer being conserved through public education, what remains is only the value-system of secular humanism. Our culture as a whole is thus terribly weakened. Moreover, the consequences of the pursuit of intense sex experiences, drug episodes, and materialism are sometimes physically and more often spiritually fatal. How tragic when students have their faith demolished by unrelenting humanists and entertainers who undermine parental authority and mock their "dogmatic religion." Pollster George Barna revealed that 67 percent of Americans do not believe there is absolute truth, but he also alarmingly reported that 52 percent of evangelical Christians responded the same way.[9]

By far the greatest cost of cultural radicalism has been exacted from disintegrating families. Society's acceptance of relativism and individualism, portrayed and subtly advanced through the media, has led to practices that can demolish the marriage bond: use of pornography, permissive sex, and no-fault divorce. What will it take to restore the life-long, faithful marriage of a man and woman as America's most honored lifestyle? What will it take to restore respect for parental values so that children will ignore the siren lure of heavy metal or rap music which centers on satanism, suicide, deviant sex, drug usage, or sadomasochism?

I remember D. James Kennedy suggesting, more than a decade ago, that in our nation the cold air mass of unbelief had collided with the warm air mass of Christianity, producing a severe storm front. Indeed, there are two basic, divergent systems of thought. One begins with God, but the other proudly revels in unaided human intellect, assuming that religion is hopelessly "backward, medieval, embarrassing or irrelevant."[10] The Apostle Paul contrasts those views:

> Where is the wise man? Where is the scholar?
> Where is the philosopher of this age? Has not
> God made foolish the wisdom of the world?
> For since in the wisdom of God the world

through its wisdom did not know him, God was pleased through the foolishness of what was preached to save those who believe.

We do, however, speak a message of wisdom among the mature, but not the wisdom of this age or of the rulers of this age, who are coming to nothing. No, we speak of God's secret wisdom, a wisdom that has been hidden and that God destined for our glory before time began. None of the rulers of this age understood it, for if they had, they would not have crucified the Lord of glory (1 Corinthians 1:20-21, 2:6-8).

Insofar as thought-leaders continue to rebel against the Judeo-Christian principles commonly accepted by the Founders, our nation is in increasing peril. As much as evangelicals deplore the cultural crisis, they do discern its source: "For our struggle is not against flesh and blood, but against the rulers, against the authorities, against the powers of this dark world" (Ephesians 6:12).

BATTLEFIELDS IN THE CULTURE WAR

To comprehend the progress of the culture war, look at several fronts where cultural radicalism is attacking cultural conservatism. Battles are being fought over radical feminism, abortion rights, arts funding, and homosexual rights.

• *Radical feminism* must be distinguished from feminism in general. All of us should applaud the many breakthroughs women have achieved in our time, affirming their equal dignity and opportunity with men. Legitimate feminism squares with

the biblical assurance of equal worth before God: "There is neither Jew nor Greek, slave nor free, male nor female, for you are
all one in Christ Jesus" (Galatians 3:20).

On the other hand, when we understand the implications of
the so-called patriarchal oppression resented by many feminists,
we realize that radical feminism is a blunt rejection of the will of
the Creator who made male and female, and who stipulated the
nature of the marriage relationship. "The bottom line of the
Feminist agenda is this," wrote one of their number, "For
women to be liberated they must be relieved of the responsibility
of childcare; the nuclear family must metamorphose."[11]

Beyond insisting that the sex/gender system is crucial and
that women must break away from male domination by controlling their own reproduction and work role, radical feminism is
capsuled in the resentful aphorism, "A woman needs a man like a
fish needs a bicycle." In feminist literature one finds suggestions
for abolishing marriage, preferring bisexuality or androgyny, and
hoping for the day when science will make it possible for women
to impregnate one another.[12]

Following radical feminism can lead to astonishing behavior.
In 1983, the New York City Council passed an ordinance requiring public places selling alcoholic beverages to post warnings that
drinking while pregnant can cause birth defects. The president of
the New York chapter of the National Organization for Women
shocked Mayor Ed Koch by her letter urging him to veto the
ordinance. She complained of "discrimination" in singling out
pregnant women as a class, and then objected to "protecting the
unborn at the expense of women's freedom."[13] NOW's national
office refused to verify or deny that the New York letter represented the organization's official position—one of morally bank-
rupt reasoning.

A feminist, criticizing radical feminism in *Christianity Today*,[14] argued that "feminism has degenerated into a phase of whining in which women are taught to see themselves as the permanently victimized under-class in a world in which everything conspires against them." The author is a lawyer and holder of a master's degree in business administration, who determined she would become a full-time mother. In her judgment, "feminism has deceived women—particularly the most talented and ambitious—leading them to despise the tasks of developing character and training children in virtue…"

Feminism is legitimately concerned about matters such as equal pay for equal work, but radical feminism flouts Judeo-Christian principles. Tragically, with the aid of the media, some of our daughters and granddaughters are being radicalized, to their own personal detriment and that of their families and nation.

• The battle over *abortion rights* involves "the greatest civil rights issue of our time and defines our national character," according to Catholic lay theologian George Weigel.[15] It is startling to realize how far our nation has drifted from its historic respect for the God-given right to life. According to Harvard professor of law Mary Ann Glendon, to find a nation "as indifferent to unborn life" as the United States, it is necessary to look beyond the West, beyond Europe, and even beyond the Soviet bloc. Only in nations such as China, where concerns about economics and population growth supersede all else, will an equally disdainful attitude toward life be found.

Paul Weyrich places this into the context of our cultural clash:

Defense of the right to life responds to such basic American values as compassion for the weak, equality of rights, and reverence for life.... Abortion is not an issue in a vacuum. It is the symbol for a cultural cleavage between those with a sense of community and responsibility and the votaries of imperial individualism; between...those who worship in churches and those who mock religion; those who accept our culture and those who seek to tear it down.[16]

To catch the full horror of the abortion "procedure," here is a description of the D & X procedure for four months or later from a 1992 seminar sponsored by the National Abortion Federation:

Guided by ultrasound, the abortionist grabs the baby's leg with forceps. The baby's leg is pulled out into the birth canal. The abortionist delivers the baby's entire body, except for the head. The abortionist jams scissors into the baby's skull. The scissors are then opened to enlarge the hole. The scissors are removed and a suction catheter is inserted. The child's brains are sucked out. The baby is then "evacuated."

It is amazing how many national leaders have changed their minds on this subject. Writing in 1971, Senator Edward Kennedy (D-MA) said that abortion was wrong. So did the Reverend Jesse Jackson in 1977. Likewise, Arkansas Governor Bill Clinton in 1986: "I am opposed to abortion and to government funding of abortions. We should not spend state funds on abortions because so many people believe abortion is wrong."[17]

The cultural radicals have been winning the popular battle over abortion, and the Supreme Court has tragically affirmed a woman's right to an abortion in its 1992 *Planned Parenthood v. Casey* ruling. Pro-abortion forces have succeeded, with the all too willing connivance of the media,[18] in reducing the issue to the question of being for or against "a woman's right to choose." Being anti-choice in and of itself is morally neutral, and often admirable. Would anyone come forward to contend that Americans should not be anti-choice on slavery, rape, or racial discrimination? To be pro-choice regarding abortion, frankly, is to be willing to snuff out an unborn child's life.

• *Government funding of the arts* sparked a fierce firefight during the years of the Bush Administration, and it is not over yet. In a meeting with the president in the west wing of the White House in the spring of 1989, I have good reason to believe I was the first person to call to his attention a work by Andres Serrano. When I described his "art," a photograph of a crucifix submerged in a jar of the artist's own urine, the president's facial expression indicated his extreme distaste. What made the matter incredible, however, was the funding of Serrano's work by taxpayers' dollars, through a grant from the National Endowment for the Arts (NEA).

I did not simply vent my spleen regarding Serrano, but reminded President Bush that before long he would need to appoint a director for the NEA. Would it not be important to consider his views about using the people's money to fund blasphemous and obscene art? The president gestured to an aide, instructing him to make a note to do just that.

That was only the beginning. Over the next months, we would discover that the NEA had funded live sex act performances, homoerotic displays, and other debased and depraved "art." The arts community resisted any limitations whatever, charging cultural conservatives with attempts to censor their creativity. One columnist imagined the liberal elite boasting, "You pathetic peasants. We're not only going to produce works which offend your deepest sensibilities, but we'll force you to pay for them as well."

Underwritten by NEA funding, one male performer urinated into a toilet on stage. What the media did not report was that he had placed a picture of our Lord Jesus Christ in that toilet. Imagine a different photograph. Would the black community have taken it lying down if the picture had Martin Luther King Jr.'s image on it? Hardly. But we evangelicals are supposed to keep quiet.

Back to the White House in 1990, where this book opened. Knowing now about the earlier Serrano episode, what I said after the "Gay Nineties" discussion was not surprising. "Mr. President, many of us find your administration's support for NEA grants underwriting sacrilegious and salacious art perplexing. We wonder if your staff may have sheltered you from seeing and knowing what is so offensive to us. If that is the case..." The president interrupted, with a curt edge to his voice: "Well, I've always been opposed to censorship." I agreed. "We all are opposed to censorship, Mr. President, but in these matters we are talking about sponsorship."

With that, I handed across the conference table a plain brown envelope, explaining: "This contains more than a dozen glossy photographs from the Mapplethorpe homoerotic art exhibit, funded by our tax dollars." I lowered my voice. "It pains me to hand something like this to the president of the United States, but you need to know." Fortunately, the president did not open the envelope then and there. All of us would have been dreadfully embarrassed. Nor did chief of staff John Sununu snatch it from him when he carried it back to the Oval Office. I have reason to believe that President George Bush and his vice president looked at the pictures together and were shocked. But NEA policies did not begin to change until sometime after the forced resignation of NEA chairman John Frohnmayer.

Ken Myers is probably correct. The cultural chasm in America today may be so wide that cultural radicals cannot comprehend why pornographic or blasphemous art is so troublesome to cultural conservatives, much less the funding of it with their tax dollars. "If Jesse Helms and Don Wildmon were shocked on first seeing 'Piss Christ', the art community, which takes such work for granted, was just as shocked that anyone minded, like perplexed cannibals wondering why the missionaries want to tamper with their menu."[19]

• Finally, *Homosexual Rights* are provoking the bitterest and most prolonged battle of all. National Gay & Lesbian Talk Force leader Jeffrey Levi was frank in his 1987 address before the National Press Club. He demanded passage of a federal gay and lesbian civil rights bill:

> But our agenda is becoming broader than that; we are no longer seeking just a right to privacy and a right to protection from wrong. We also have a right—as heterosexual Americans have already—to see government and society affirm our lives. Now that is a statement that may make some of our liberal friends queasy. But the truth is, until our relationships are recog-

nized in the law—through domestic partner legislation or the definition of beneficiary, for example—until we are provided the same financial incentives in tax law and government programs to encourage our family relationships, then we will not have achieved equality in American society.[20]

With the collaboration of media and academic elites determined to be "politically correct," the homosexual movement has made huge progress en route to its real goal—full cultural acceptance. As one step, anti-discrimination laws lift homosexual acts to a special level of protection, at the same time stamping religious opponents as the ones guilty of antagonistic and immoral behavior.

Brilliantly, but diabolically, homosexuals have chosen their terminology precisely. To avoid being described by what they do, which is gross and unnatural, they insist on being called gay rather than homosexual. To make it appear that they have no choice in the matter, they insist on speaking about their sexual orientation rather than preference. To put those who disagree with their lifestyle or politics in the worst light, they insist on labeling them homophobes. And, they then brazenly charge that homophobes are guilty of supporting heterosexism—the notion that heterosexuality is morally superior to homosexuality.[21]

Homosexuals have made remarkable gains in recent years. They have managed to make AIDS a politically protected disease, giving it more of a civil rights privacy emphasis than that of a public health issue. Yet in September 1994, a specialist in infectious diseases opened "60 Minutes" saying: "We are now in the midst of the world's worst epidemic [carried by] the most serious germ that the globe has ever experienced. And it's the first time in the history of public health or medicine that a disease has been treated as a secret disease." As gay rights activists seek protection from discrimination, many avoid diagnostic testing of any sort. What is one price of deliberate refusal to learn if one has the HIV virus? Another physician warned: "If we know [by testing] that the mother is HIV-positive and the infant is too, we will not lose the child in the first month. If we don't know, the baby dies."

Gay activists have lied to themselves and to the youth of America that condoms provide "safe sex." Many parents can testify that, as a birth control device, condoms are not fail-safe. They are inadequate even among adults deliberately trying to avoid pregnancy. Columnist Cal Thomas quotes the editor of *Rubber Chemistry and Technology:*

> The rubber comprising latex condoms has intrinsic voids about 5 microns in size. Since this is roughly 10 times smaller than sperm, the latter are effectively blocked in ideal circumstances..... Contrarily, the AIDS virus is only 0.1 microns in size. Since this is a factor of 50 smaller than the voids inherent in rubber, the virus can readily pass through the condom should it find such a passage.[22]

The U.S. Army's top AIDS researcher, Dr. Robert Redfield, says that "Common sense tells me that condoms fail, and when they fail, human beings lose their lives."[23] Distribution of condoms in schools or anywhere else implies that they are medically recommended. Redfield believes that message is both dishonest and deadly.

Columnist Joseph Sobran suggests that "fighting AIDS with

condoms is like fighting lung cancer with filter tips. If any other product were to fail so frequently, putting the user so much at risk, Ralph Nader would be calling press conferences to demand that the federal government clamp down on the whole industry. The goal of safe-sexers is not to save lives, but to save the sexual revolution.[24]

Homosexual activists criticize the media for focusing on the weird elements of their movement. On the other hand, television networks cleaned up their coverage of the 1993 gay "March on Washington," wanting to portray homosexuals as ordinary people. Only C-Span cable viewers saw the unedited nudity, blasphemy, and all-around vulgarity that characterized the demonstration—while police, who should have been making arrests, looked the other way. And few Americans realize that homosexuals celebrate the diversity of their coalition, demanding acceptance of every sub-group, including sadomasochists, drag queens, and even pedophiles. The movement flaunts bizarre and degenerate behavior. Indeed, the word lifestyle is a misnomer. More often than not, homosexual behavior is a "deathstyle."

It is unthinkable that gays could throw some denominations into turmoil by demanding ordination to the ministry. Worse yet, in 1988 and in 1992 they secured support for their agenda from all potential Democratic presidential nominees. But the most significant part of their battle in the culture war was fought in the District of Columbia.

GAY RIGHTS VERSUS RELIGIOUS FREEDOM

In 1988, homosexuals employed a District of Columbia human rights statute to force Roman Catholic Georgetown University to grant space and funds to a gay rights group on campus. After a two-year effort, thanks to the leadership of Sen. Bill Armstrong

(R-CO), Congress carved out an exemption for church-affiliated schools, through the appropriations bill, to let them decide for themselves whether they would give money or recognition to groups promoting or condoning homosexuality. Twice during the battle NAE pulled together a press conference, with a broad supporting coalition, to urge passage of the Armstrong amendment and to clarify that this was a religious liberty issue, not a matter of gay-bashing.

In press conference statements, I suggested that requiring Georgetown to fund gay rights advocates made as much sense as compelling Hebrew Union College to fund a campus chapter of a neo-Nazi group, or the black Howard University to support a chapter of the Ku Klux Klan.

No conflict better illustrates the clash between cultural conservatives and cultural radicals. Stripped of all emotion and posturing, the issue is this: Can a religious school be forced to subsidize groups promoting beliefs and practices contrary to its religious convictions? Roman Catholic Georgetown University forthrightly believes homosexual acts and advocacy to be sin.

Sad to say, while cultural conservatives won this time, about one-third of the senators and representatives revealed by their votes that they preferred gay rights over religious freedom. They would have been willing to force Georgetown to underwrite the expenses for students to promote homosexuality. What if their kind of thinking should become the majority mind-set in the Congress of the United States?

Pressure for gay rights never seems to let up. Senator Armstrong again had to do battle in the summer of 1990, when the District government required organizations like Big Brothers and Girl Scouts to admit homosexuals into their ranks as counselors, coaches, and leaders. Armstrong finally prevailed, after losing the first time around, when the Senate by 54-45 decided that such organizations should have the right to exclude homosexuals as role models if they wished to do so. The frightening aspect of the vote was that this time the minority believing that youth organizations should be required to include homosexuals in leadership had grown to forty-five out of one hundred.

I have come to a harsh conclusion. There is no greater threat to the survival of our culture today than the insidious and unrelenting drive for homosexual rights. Aided and abetted by radical feminism, propagandized and rationalized by media and academic elites, the gay rights movement is obstinately resolved to destroy the traditional family and thus American society as we know it.

In the civil new war of the nineties, government must uphold conservative cultural values if our society is to endure. Tragically, the federal government's resolve has conspicuously weakened. Cultural radicals are winning many battles on these and other fronts. The prognosis for America does not seem bright.

Even so, consider this moving incident discovered by Alistair Cooke in the records of the Connecticut House of Representatives:

> The time was the 19th of May, 1780. The place was Hartford, Connecticut. The day had gone down in New England history as a terrible foretaste of Judgment Day. For at noon the skies turned from blue to gray and by mid-afternoon had blackened over so densely that, in that religious age, men fell on their knees and begged a final blessing before the end

came. The Connecticut House of Representatives was in session. And as some men fell
down and others clamored for an immediate
adjournment, the Speaker of the House, one
Colonel Davenport, came to his feet. He
silenced them and said these words: "The Day
of Judgment is either approaching or it is not. If
it is not, there is no cause for adjournment. If it
is, I choose to be found doing my duty. I wish,
therefore, that candles may be brought."[25]

Evangelicals must be found doing their duty. The question
at the beginning of this chapter demands an answer: Who will
determine America's future?

Ronald Reagan was fond of saying, "The greatest revolution
in history began with the words, 'We the people.'" But those
were the events of 1776 and 1787. Today, the greatest recapturing, the greatest renewal, the greatest revival of a nation in history
will have to begin with the words, "We, God's people."

WHAT MUST GOD'S PEOPLE DO?

This is the time for evangelicals to grip history's helm, to chart
their nation's course. The goal is not to construct a Christian
America. However, with everything in me I urge that we remain
"one nation under God." That ambition will survive the scrutiny
of the Supreme Court, for "we are a religious people whose institutions presuppose a Supreme Being" (*Zorach v. Clauson*, 1952).

I concur with Charles Colson that America is not now, nor
was it ever, a Christian nation in the common use of the term.
Colson suggests that the word "nation" can be understood on
three different levels, as the *people*, the *government*, or the *culture*

of a country.[26] Not even in colonial times, when church membership was below 10 percent, has a majority of our people been
committed Christians. Our government was not constituted as a
Christian nation, and the First Amendment specifically prohibits
establishing a state church. Only as a culture can we fairly refer to
America as a Christian nation. Indeed, our ideals and morals
were shaped by the Christian faith.

ADDING UP OUR ASSETS

If and when evangelicals decide to do political battle for their
culture, they will be surprised to find millions of cultural conservatives—whether they call themselves that or not—willing to
follow. Evangelicals have sufficient *reason*, adequate *resources*, and
every *right* to take the political lead.

Christians have multiple reasons to engage in the political
life of the nation in an unprecedented way. Above all, they
believe in an Almighty God who judges nations. They are well
aware, for example, that God will not forever tolerate a homosexual culture (Genesis 18-19, Romans 1, 2 Peter 2, Jude). More
and more they grasp the gravity of the current crisis, and they
know that God is honored when his people work for righteousness in society. They have every reason to believe that God can
multiply their efforts just as surely as Jesus miraculously multiplied a boy's lunch of bread and fish to feed five thousand.

Evangelicals clearly have resources to exert a decisive influence upon this nation. To counter cultural radicalism, there are
more than twelve hundred Christian radio stations, increasing
numbers with a talk-radio format, and about 450 Christian television stations in the country. Thirty million people, according
to researcher George Barna, read Christian magazines regularly.

Associated Press religion writer George Cornell reported that
giving to churches and religious organizations in 1992 totaled

56.7 billion, about fourteen times the $4 billion spent on professional baseball, football, and basketball. He estimated that cumulative church attendance during 1993 was 5.6 billion, fifty-five times greater than the 103 million total attendance in the three major sports leagues. That means that more people are in church or synagogue on an average weekend than attend those professional sports events all year.[27] Further, there are nearly ninety colleges in the Christian College Coalition, producing graduates who can lead, and probably over two million children are enrolled in Christian schools from kindergarten through grade twelve.

George Gallup asserts that "America is unique in the world for the high levels of religious belief among its educated people." His mid-1990 research shows that 45 percent of Americans describe themselves as evangelicals, or born-again Christians. Gallup explains that some people may be hesitant to use those terms of themselves, but that "alternatively worded questions have yielded similar results." High percentages hold conservative theological views regarding the divinity of Christ or his resurrection from the dead. Even allowing for exaggeration, although Gallup's reputation as a pollster is impeccable, evangelicals have the potential political resources to change the nation.

They also have the spiritual resources. Their confidence in the sovereignty of God was bolstered by the crumbling of communism in Eastern Europe in 1989. With George Washington, they believe in "the invisible hand that conducts the affairs of men." With ancient Israel's kings, they believe that "the battle is the Lord's" (1 Samuel 17:14).

Happily, evangelicals also have the right to advance their convictions in the public square. They cannot be gerrymandered out of the political arena because they bring religious beliefs into the battle. Under the Constitution, with full freedom to wield their rights as citizens, they will do well to recall a vivid biblical image: "See, I have placed before you an open door that no one can shut" (Revelation 3:8).

Comparatively low voter turnout in recent decades can play into the hands of evangelicals, provided they mobilize their constituency better than others. After all, the value of a vote is relative to the total number of votes cast. To illustrate, 24,000 voted in my 1976 primary election in Colorado, while 240,000 voted in November. A primary vote in September thus had ten times the clout of a vote in November. Further, America has never had as high a percentage of older people as it has today. These folks are most likely to have conservative cultural values, and, they go to the polls in greater percentages than any other age group. On the other hand, the eighteen-to-twenty-four generation "knows less, cares less, and reads newspapers less" than any generation in the last fifty years.[28] Especially vulnerable to the individualistic, relativistic, and hedonistic spirit of the times, it is fortunate that, unlike their elders, they send a low percentage of their number to the polls.

Himself an evangelical, Doug Wead was an advisor to presidential candidate George Bush, a member of his White House transition team, and then for almost two years special assistant to the president in public liaison. In 1992 he was asked, "Do politicians take evangelicals any more seriously these days?" I resonate with his off-the-cuff but candid answer:

> I think they kind of treat the evangelical movement like a seven-foot-tall high schooler who can't play basketball. If he ever learns how to play, he's going to be awesome. In the meantime, they'll do everything they can to take

advantage of his awkwardness.... Evangelicals
can generate more mail, more phone calls, than
any other group. We've always known that.
Our predecessors told us that. Evangelicals have
the numbers. But...[29]

We must admit that evangelicals have been awkward.[30]
Literally the sole political act of millions of individual
Christians—aside from voting—has been to sign a certain
anonymous petition and mail it to the Federal Communications
Commission to protest Madalyn Murray O'Hair's efforts to get
all religious broadcasting off the air. When I suggest that there
are a few small problems with that petition, I speak sarcastically.
First, O'Hair was never involved in it. Second, it was not drawn
up to remove religious broadcasting from the airwaves. Third,
the petition was resolved satisfactorily by the FCC in August
1975. That's not a typo—1975 is the correct year.

Those sincere Christians were misinformed. Somebody lied
to them. The FCC never has been able to turn off the spigot
from which the petitions flowed, and the total is climbing
toward 30 million. Think of the wasted postage, the unnecessary
federal expense in handling the mail, and the useless paper going
into a landfill.

While there's a real culture war being fought, millions of
well-meaning Christians have been playing a make-believe game.
On the other hand, evangelicals give promise of becoming awesome. Serious candidates for public office are being spawned in
prayer meetings, rather than smoke-filled rooms. Telephones
ring off the hook on Capitol Hill when critical issues are being
debated in Congress. Christian Citizenship ministries in local
churches are providing dependable educational materials so that

God's people can decide how to vote. If certain Members of Congress vote against funding for religious child care while voting for funding of homoerotic art, as has actually happened, evangelicals are learning about it in a timely fashion, when that information is particularly valuable. In many states and localities, evangelicals have even taken over political party organizations.

Evangelicals are being developed by good coaches. This book, as a matter of fact, is designed to help that seven-footer become coordinated and fulfill his awesome potential.

The elections of 1980, 1984, and 1992 demonstrated the impact of an identifiable evangelical vote. No longer can the media treat conservative Christians like the Rodney Dangerfield of American politics. Media respect is evidenced by the ferocity of the attacks against evangelicals.

THE ULTIMATE FACTOR

Consider a theoretical future presidential election where one candidate genuinely supports culturally conservative values while the other turns his back on evangelical concerns. Let's assume George Gallup's more modest figures, that evangelicals represent 20 percent of the electorate. If 75 percent of those evangelicals cast ballots while only half of the non-evangelicals do, evangelicals would control over 27 percent of the total vote, not just their usual 20 percent.

Once more, cutting the margin closer, project the impact of a 60 percent evangelical vote against 50 percent for the rest. Then evangelicals would own 23 percent of the total, not just 20 percent. That extra 3 percent may not seem like much, but it could have changed the outcome of four presidential elections since World War II. If the lion's share of it had been given to the loser, in 1948 Thomas E. Dewey would have defeated Harry

Truman. In 1960, John F. Kennedy would have lost to Richard Nixon. In 1968, it would have pushed Hubert Humphrey past Richard Nixon. And in 1976 it would have returned Gerald Ford to the Oval Office, rather than Jimmy Carter.

In that light, one development in the 1994 elections looms larger than any other. For the first time in modern political history, evangelicals voted in larger percentages than the non-evangelical population. What a gratifying turnabout—something I have literally been "preaching" since my own run for Congress in 1976. Compared to Gallup's 20 percent baseline, the Times Mirror Center for People and the Press said that evangelicals constituted 27 percent of the total vote, and the University of Akron's Bliss Center for Applied Politics research said the figure was 33 percent.

It is not therefore surprising that six of ten challengers on the Democrats' list of "most dangerous radical religious right" unseated incumbents. One new member of Congress tells me that 30-35 of his fellow representatives are evangelicals. Many have come from hitherto unrepresented evangelical denominations such as Assemblies of God, Christian & Missionary Alliance, General Baptist, International Church of the Foursquare Gospel, and United Brethren in Christ.

There is no doubt in my mind that evangelical Christians can still win the culture war, by electing courageous leaders with moral character, political competence, and godly values. That will come about through the many avenues outlined in this book, but mostly through the great spiritual weapon of prayer and the great political weapon of the vote. Whether cultural conservatives will win depends in great measure upon their spiritual leaders, for "If the trumpet does not sound a clear call, who will get ready for battle?" (1 Corinthians 14:8).

For those leaders and their nation, Carl Henry has a sobering prophetic word:

> Can Western civilization escape inner chaos and self-destruction if it faces the future without a significant role for transcendent justice and the revealed will of God? If you think not—as I think not—then your Christian commitment imposes upon you a heavy duty to share in the present effort to preserve the American republic and to warn and instruct all the modern powers that are marching off the map to join once-great nations of antiquity in their oblivion.[31]

What else can be said to a culture hell-bent toward its own destruction? This nation has a momentous choice. If it refuses to be one nation under God, it will assuredly be one nation under judgment.

POSTSCRIPT

AT LEAST I TRIED!

If decent people do not like
the way politicians behave,
they should either get into politics
or refrain from complaining
about anything politicians do.
—Teddy Roosevelt

July 4, 1976, was the 200th anniversary of America's Declaration of Independence. It was a perfect year to run for Congress. September 14, two months and ten days later, was of no historic significance, except to a few dozen candidates hoping to snare a nomination in Colorado's primary elections. I was among them.

I was hoping to become a member of the U.S. House of Representatives. But first I would have to secure the Republican nomination in Colorado's second congressional district by defeating Ed Scott, the odds-on favorite.

I busied myself in the office, endured a bit of nervousness, and berated the rainy afternoon, complete with hailstorm, which was sure to cut voter turnout.

Several dozen friends accepted our invitation to share the evening with us, to snack, talk, and above all watch the returns on television. Deep down, I suspect, they somehow knew that they would be needed to play the role of comforters, even though our gathering was offIcially billed as a victory party.

As the ringing phones became more insistent, the moment of truth closed in. Was I ready to make a statement? The *Denver*

Post wanted to know. No, not yet. Denver's NBC-TV anchor was on the line wondering why not. Why not? Well, the absentee ballots hadn't even been counted. Maybe they would counter the early evening's trend and turn the race around.

Looking back I'm surprised I didn't hear it more often: "What's a nice pastor like you doing in a place like politics?" To many folks, politics is just one thing: dirty. What self-respecting Christian—much less a pastor—would let himself get involved in politics?

For one, I would. My chief allegiance in life is to Jesus Christ. Two millennia ago, didn't he make it clear that his method would be to send his followers into the world, as his Father had sent him? God deliberately sent his Son from the purity of heaven into a dirty, polluted, and decadent world. Jesus' birth in a stable—not the beautiful, antiseptic scene pictured on our Christmas cards, but a smelly, dirty barn with manure on the floor—symbolized that.

It seemed consistent to me that God would put his people in the so-called dirty world of politics. Like Jesus, they would enter that world on assignment, to bring truth, justice, righteousness, and even redemption.

And hadn't Jesus himself called Christians "the salt of the earth" (Matthew 5:13)? He was not simply suggesting that his followers should flavor society. In the pre-refrigeration days of the first century, salt was used as a preservative. To protect a catch of fish or a fresh kill from spoilage, one should salt it well. If Christian "salt" is to fulfill its function, it must be shaken out of the "saltshaker" of the Church. To preserve society from moral and spiritual corruption, that salt must be shaken into every crevice of the culture. Especially important are the decision-making structures at all levels—local, county, state, and national.

Churches that withdraw from the world or monopolize their people's loyalties and thus deprive them of optional time to serve in the world unwittingly foil their Lord's purpose for the Church.

Christian laymen are desperately needed in politics. So are Christian women. But pastors? Don't they have a lifetime call to the ministry? How dare they turn their backs on God's calling And yet there I was, campaigning for political office.

In my case, the "what's a nice pastor like you doing in politics?" question seemed especially severe. As far back as the fourth grade, I went on record as headed for the ministry. In high school I took four years of Latin, believing that such a foundation would make Greek come easier in college. It did. That in turn made it possible to take Hebrew my first year in seminary All along, I knew exactly where I was headed.

That's why resigning the pastorate of my suburban Denver church in early 1975 to run for Congress, of all things, might well have been challenged by somebody with the guts to do it But nobody did.

My road to the campaign trail began in 1973. A lobbyist friend introduced me to the Senate president, who in turn invited me to serve as Senate chaplain for a week in March and then another in May. Playing golf with two senators one day, I suggested a Bible study among the legislators. It should be private and unpublicized, I thought, and if no one else were available to lead it, they were looking at a volunteer.

Early that December, Sen. Hugh Fowler invited me to lunch. Unknown to me, he was chairman of the Senate committee that hired the staff. His committee, he said, hoped that I would be willing to become the regular Senate chaplain for 1974. For years they had operated with a visiting-fireman approach, with dozens of ministers, priests, or rabbis visiting the Senate for a day or two or as much as a week. How much better it would be if their chaplain could be there every day, developing friendships and helping meet the needs of the senators and their staffs!

"I would love to," I replied, "provided that I wouldn't be limited to the formal duty of opening the sessions with prayer, as important as that would be."

"That's exactly why we're asking you," he shot back. "When we were playing golf, I became aware how really interested you were in us senators." When Hugh finally introduced me to the staff, he told them, "He's your pastor, whenever you need him." My tenure as chaplain would continue through the 1975 session. Those were great, thoroughly enjoyable days.

There's a political maxim that says, "If you like baloney and love the law, you should never go see either one made." But I found it unreliable. Day by day I watched the law being made, from a seat on the leather bench surrounding the beautiful, almost elegant Senate chamber, with its clear-windowed view to the Rocky Mountains just a few miles west. I was impressed, fascinated. How in this world could law-making be done better than by representative government?

I realized I could fit into this kind of scene—and wanted to. But because my interests were in national rather than state issues, Congress, not the legislature, would be my goal. I took the leap in January 1975, resigning my five-year pastorate to run for Congress. The last week in February I flew to Washington to reconnoiter. Frankly, I didn't even realize I should have gone to the Republican National Committee to inform them of my interest in running. However, one contact led to another, and I secured appointments with Congressmen John Conlan of

Arizona, Clarence Brown of Ohio, Guy VanderJagt of Michigan, John Buchanan of Alabama, and others. But the most memorable meeting took place with Sen. Mark Hatfield of Oregon.

His personal secretary emerged from the inner office with an apology and the senator's datebook. What a shame. An emergency required him to return to Oregon that night. The remaining three days of work and appointments had to be compressed into Wednesday. He really wanted to see me, but it might be impossible. If I went to the meeting of the Senate Rules Committee, however, we would at least bump into each other for a minute. It was twenty-five minutes before I could shoehorn myself into the hearing room. The closest Senate election in history had been dumped into the Senate's lap by the state of New Hampshire, whose Governor's Ballot Committee was unwilling or unable to declare a winner. Republican Louis Wyman originally appeared to win by 355 votes, but the Secretary of State's recount produced a reversal, with Democrat John Durkin ahead by ten votes. Taking another look, New Hampshire officials said that Wyman had won after all, by a total of two ballots. The Constitution had a provision for this kind of situation. The Senate, the final judge of the qualifications of its members, would have to decide.

Shortly after I found a seat in the hearing room, the committee moved to send its chairman, Sen. Howard Cannon, and its ranking minority member, Senator Hatfield, to the basement vault where approximately thirty-five hundred disputed paper ballots were stored, to bring them into the light of committee scrutiny. As the television lights snapped off, Mark Hatfield moved from the dais, spotted me, and invited me along for the ride.

Crowding the elevator were the two senators, attorneys for both claimants of the seat, about eight or ten Capitol police, and I. After successive vault doors were opened, several very ordinary, used cardboard cartons containing the disputed ballots were loaded onto a rolling cart for the trip upward. I glanced at the ballots as they were spread out on the committee's table. It seemed incredible that so many people could not follow simple directions: to vote with an X, not a check or other symbol; to make sure that the arms of the X crossed within the circle, and nowhere else. Their carelessness or orneriness had muddied up the outcome of an election to the United States Senate.

Senator Hatfield interrupted my reverie. Could we go into a quiet anteroom for a few minutes, so that we could at least talk briefly? Knowing that I wanted to discuss the feasibility of running and to pick up some pointers, Mark nevertheless had some things he wanted to mention first.

"You're going to be in an entirely new arena, unlike the church," he said. "Because some people think clergymen have their feet planted firmly in the air and aren't real human beings, your advisers will want to establish your image. 'Bob,' one may say, 'we know you wouldn't tell any really raunchy jokes to this men's group today, but how about a couple of slightly off-color stories to let 'em know you're one of the boys?' "

For a moment, this senator turned the tables on me. He was the pastor and I his parishioner. Drawing himself to attention and pointing his finger, he spoke forcefully: "Never do that. Never forget who you are as a man of God. It's not worth losing your character to win an election." He then gave me his formula for life's priorities. My first loyalty must always be to the Lord; my second to my family; and only my third to my constituents.

Who wouldn't be pumped up after a week of such meetings? The members of Congress seemed to be saying that I would be an attractive candidate, that I could win, and that they were eager to have me as a colleague in the House of Representatives. I believed them. And I flew back to Colorado elated, convinced I should run.

How does one get started running for Congress? Obviously, I needed to learn how the political process worked. I needed to meet my party's top leaders and cultivate party contacts. I had to develop a broad set of political convictions. And without question I needed to become widely known in my congressional district. But before that, I had to settle a preliminary question. Can anybody get elected to Congress without first holding a lower office? A search through that year's *Almanac of American Politics* showed that about one-third of the members of the House were holding their initial political office. No barrier there.

You can't go far without a campaign manager. Late in 1975 we found him, thanks to a mutual friend in the state Senate. Jim Files was a professor at Denver University but in a position to put a healthy part-time effort into my campaign. He had already successfully managed a Texas congressional campaign for Bob Price. Unfortunately, my name was not as adaptable to a winning slogan as the Texan's "Price is right."

In many states, anybody can get on the ballot by obtaining a petition with a certain number of signatures, but Colorado's nominating system involves a caucus and convention process. Since caucuses meet every other year, I discovered to my chagrin that in my six years of residence I'd passed up all three opportunities to attend a caucus in my precinct.

Several secretly sympathetic party officials brought me up to speed. In my own Jefferson County, they even gave me much-appreciated exposure to party workers by allowing me to train them in special seminars. Over the months, there would be no end of Republican county or state central committee meetings and the like.

Several hundred Republican delegates to June's Second Congressional District Assembly would decide who would have a place on the ballot. The majority would be party veterans who managed to get themselves appointed year after year. I spent countless evenings visiting delegates from the prior year's list. I was impressed with the high caliber of many of those people. They were highly motivated and unselfish, committed to better government, not stereotypical political hacks.

By one means or another, I got acquainted with the top leadership. I tackled rumored rivals for the nomination by inviting them to lunch. I spent time developing my political views. With a conservative political philosophy to systematize my positions, I took to research like a duck to water. There were exams along the way. I spent two tough hours with the Paul Revere Committee, an ultra-conservative group that would brook little variation from its hard-line positions. Another night in a candidate forum, one questioner demanded a simple yes or no answer to eight complex questions from each of the four candidates. I'll guarantee that he got more than his requested thirty-two one-word responses.

It was a perpetual effort to become known in the community. I had a modest starting point as Senate chaplain and the former pastor of Trinity Baptist Church in suburban Wheat Ridge. Since I was representing the National Association of Evangelicals' relief and development arm, World Relief, on a part-time basis, I spoke in many churches of varied denominations. Of course, I was careful that my message not be political in any way. In that bicentennial year, Rotary, Kiwanis, and Optimist Clubs were more than open to a patriotic speech.

Seemingly endless neighborhood coffees were a great way to meet people and enlist support. The press began to seek interviews. Radio spots were simple to make and television commercials were no problem, given that marvelous device called a teleprompter. And parades. I never knew there were so many in all the communities in the district. We tried not to miss walking in any of them those summer Saturdays, especially when surrounded by our teenage daughter and her friends, wearing our campaign colors and carrying banners. Freshly scrubbed and pretty as could be, they were a great attraction. There was another plus in those parades: the first British double-decker bus imported to Colorado, dedicated to Bob Dugan for Congress, the contribution of a Boulder entrepreneur.

But our basic strategy was to take our campaign to the homes of the people by walking. There's no way to calculate the thousands of homes I personally visited as a candidate, most often with my wife walking the opposite side of the street. When folks were not home, we left a brochure with a short handwritten note. The campaign ran through the hottest months of the year, yielding an unexpected bonus—we walked ourselves into excellent physical shape.

A serious run for Congress is no lark. It takes extraordinary commitment. For me, the price tallied up to twenty months of my life and about $50,000, some of it in unreimbursed travel and meal expenses, but most of it in lost income. At today's salaries, the bill might have been five times that amount. A check of income tax returns shows an adjusted gross income for our family of $5,108 in 1975 and $8,513 in 1976. Our modest income was generated only by Lynne's part-time retail sales work and my per diem arrangement with World Relief.

Lynne, Bob (20), and Cheri (18) paid a good part of the price of my running. In fact, one's immediate family are the backers any political candidate needs most. Lynne was totally supportive. When it was over, our son, Bob III, observed that the campaign had strengthened us, bringing our family together in a wonderful way. What can you say about a son who would press into his dad's hand a political contribution of $350? As my father says, there are times when you feel like you're swallowing golf balls. And what can you say about a daughter like Cheri, who put off going to college because she wanted to help her dad's campaign?

I was the first to announce, doing so in a press conference at the state capitol on January 5, 1976. That day I learned some useful lessons about the media. One television reporter arrived early and entertained himself by trying to unnerve me. "Why," he demanded, "are you using this large committee room instead of the official press room across the hall?" I explained that we needed the larger room because a hundred of my friends would be coming to witness the announcement. "A press conference is for the press," he bullied, "not for the public. Besides, the lighting's better in that room, and I'm going to have to change my film if you insist we meet in here." As other press arrived, I heard him grumbling, "You'd think he was announcing for president of the United States."

I saw the fruit of his irritation that night on the ten o'clock news. As the anchorman gave a brief report of my announcement, a picture of me appeared in the upper left corner of the screen. Of thousands of frames of film, channel 7 chose one where I was moistening my lips. I looked like a freak with three lips. But the race was on.

Caucus attendance the first Monday in May broke records that year. The Ford-Reagan contest for the presidential nomination was in full swing, and the crowded caucuses insured that a handful of insiders could not routinely renominate incumbents. Among other things, the caucuses, open to party members living within the precinct, would elect delegates to the congressional district assembly. More than half of the fifty-one who turned out in my precinct favored my candidacy, so I had my first small taste of political victory.

The rules at the June assembly were simple. To secure a place on the ballot, a candidate must receive at least 20 percent of the delegate votes. The one with the highest percentage would have the ballot's top line for the September 14 primary. Two contestants for the nomination had dropped out before the assembly, leaving just Ed and me, but the politically experienced Scott took the top line with 65 percent. He seemed crestfallen at failing to keep me off the ballot.

The press tried to balance its coverage of the candidates, essentially giving us three days in the sun: our individual announcements, caucus night, and the nominating assembly. For weeks at a time I wondered if they had forgotten the campaign, though we occasionally got a column inch or two on page thirty-seven of the daily papers.

Toward the end, I thought we had a significant advantage. Our campaign ran a series of thirty-second TV commercials on "Good Morning America" and the "Today" show. After Labor Day, we aired four newspaper-advertised, five-minute TV spots in the evening. Ed Scott never used television. Apparently he didn't need to.

There would be no turnaround that election night. The early trends became a consistent pattern. Admitting within the room what all our friends now realized, I fielded the media calls and made concession statements. If the television crews wanted to catch me later that night, they would find me at Ed Scott's victory party.

It isn't easy to put a smile on your face, walk into your opponent's celebration, and acknowledge that he has defeated you. Our children didn't have much heart for it, but they came anyway. Cheri remembers how the TV cameras wouldn't leave her face while tears etched a path across her cheeks. Ed was the epitome of graciousness, and he positively beamed when I asked for an Ed Scott button and pinned it to my suit. I promised that we would wholeheartedly back him, and asked my workers to do the same. The next day the unofficial tally showed Scott with 17,029 votes and Dugan with 7,519. While I could euphemistically say that I had come in second while my opponent was next to last, the truth is that in one mid-September day my dream of going to Washington as a member of Congress vaporized.

Why did I lose the primary? There are several reasons:

• **I was hindered by my shortcomings as a candidate.**

That admission must come first. When Jim Files came on board as campaign manager, one of his first observations was, "We need to teach you how to think politically." How right he was. My opponent once remarked that our campaign color, green, was especially appropriate for me as a candidate.

• **I was blind-sided by party regulars.**

While I apparently was leading for the nomination, party officials were discussing the matter among themselves and seeking another candidate. They settled on Ed Scott, actively recruiting him. It would irritate me to no end to hear Scott again and again tell how he was not seeking this office, but that his "phone began ringing off the hook with people asking me to run." Hyperbole is part of politics, but a number of important party officials did encourage him to enter the race.

- **I didn't secure the help of enough Christian friends.**

One of my big hopes was to bring a host of new players into the political game from the churches. It didn't work out that way. All too often fellow Christians would shake my hand and announce, "Bob, I'm going to do for you the most important thing that one believer can do for another. I'm going to pray for you." Naturally I wanted their prayers, but I came to resent their assurances when I learned that they really meant, "Since I'm doing the most momentous thing, don't expect me to do anything else—not write you a check, not spend volunteer time in your office, not walk the precincts with your literature."

- **I was opposed by a better-known candidate.**

The party went for age and experience when it recruited Ed Scott. He had been a member of the city council and mayor of Englewood, Colorado; had served as an Arapahoe County Commissioner; and had been elected to the state Senate. Not the least of the recognition he enjoyed came from being "Sheriff Scotty" on a popular Denver children's television show, extremely well known to long-time Colorado residents.

• **I was unable to build an adequate organization.**

This is the most important factor of all. I was delayed for weeks in filing with the Federal Election Commission. For want of a campaign treasurer, I could not officially file. For want of filing, we could not begin to raise funds. One by one, three Christian friends, each a certified public accountant, took weeks to tell me he couldn't serve. Finally another friend, a non-CPA, accepted the job. Just retired, he and his wife even canceled the second month of a winter vacation in Arizona, unwilling to miss that much of the campaign. What I wouldn't have given for a few dozen more friends like that.

Losing is never fun. But do I regret the time, money, and emotional energy that went into the campaign? Not on your life. Among the millions of Americans who perpetually berate their government, few can say, "At least I tried." I can.

Even though I wasn't successful in my bid for a congressional seat, God turned that political failure into success. To our great surprise, a little over two years later my wife and I would move to the Capitol. While I would not have a congressional office on Capitol Hill, I would move into an office just three blocks from the White House—assigned to raise the profile and increase the effectiveness of the Office of Public Affairs of the National Association of Evangelicals.

In my early weeks in Washington, two congressmen in separate conversations told me I would have more influence on the nation through NAE than if I had won a seat in the House. At the time I thought they were trying to console me by saying something kind. Today I agree with their judgment.

The NAE was not well known outside religious circles in the sixties and seventies. Judging by the media, you might have thought the fabric of America's religious life was woven of just three strands: Catholic, Jewish, and Protestant. More often than not, the National Council of Churches was assumed to be the sole voice of Protestantism. Evangelicals were frustrated at being misrepresented or not being represented at all.

Today there's a world of difference. The White House, Congress, and even the Supreme Court realize there are four major strands in our religious fabric: Catholic, Jewish, ecumenical Protestant, and evangelical Protestant. Government and the media know that NAE is the institutional gathering-place for evangelicals from fifty thousand churches in over seventy denominations, and that NAE has become the major alternative to the National Council of Churches in American church life.

Over the years, God has helped us put together a competent team of professionals in Washington. Together we function much like the office of a senator, although our constituency is spread over all fifty states. Senators *respond* to the needs of their people, so do we. Senators report to the people of their state, so do we. Senators represent their state's interest before the federal government; so do we.

Having read my experience, you may not be able to imagine yourself as a candidate or member of Congress. No problem. As this book makes clear, politics is far more than running for office. Frankly, ninety-nine out of one hundred people who read this book neither have nor ever will seriously consider running for office. Nor should they. But Christians can play any number of critical roles in the pivotal world of politics—especially working to insure that "the righteous are in authority."

Having said that, I must also admit that this book is written for the one in one hundred who definitely should seek political office. Some day, I hope to hear from several members of

Congress, a governor or two, the speaker of a state legislature, a county executive, or any number of city council or school board members for whom this book was the starter.

You cannot have read this book without realizing its one major goal: to show how you can take an active, influential, and Christ-honoring role in politics.

It wouldn't suprise me at all if God is calling you.

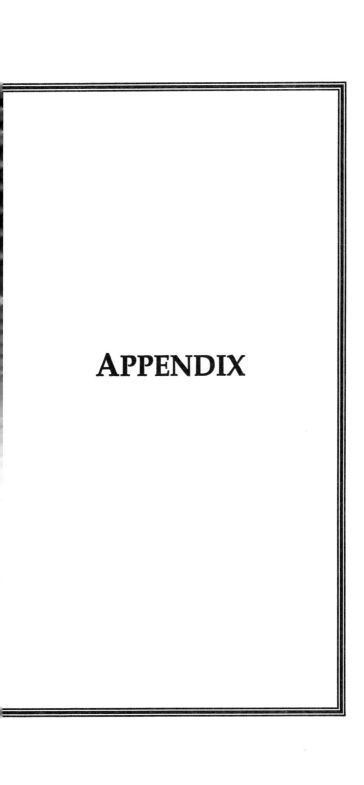

APPENDIX

HOW TO GET STARTED

A fter speaking, one of the questions I am most frequently asked is this: "How can I get started in politics?"

INVOLVEMENT

One way to get underway is to volunteer to the party of your choice. If you have a friend who is politically active, ask her to take you to the next party function and introduce you around.

Otherwise, it's easy enough to look in the phone book for your party's county organization, e.g. the Republican Party of Jefferson County or the Democratic Party of Fairfax County. Drop by for a visit, chat with the staff (most of whom are probably themselves unpaid workers), and offer your help wherever it is most needed. In the winter or early spring after an election year, the party will be filling vacancies in its structure. Your precinct may have an opening for a committeeman or woman, allowing a great opportunity to volunteer or to run for the slot, however it's done in your state. Then you will really be on the inside where you will learn by doing.

If you are a peer of the county chairman, perhaps a business or professional person, take him to lunch, let him know what motivates you to be involved, and ask him to mentor you. Parties and their chairmen have a special place in their hearts for volunteers.

The other way to begin is to offer your help to a worthy candidate whom you trust, whether running for a local office, the U.S. Senate, or president, for that matter. That could mean that you will help an incumbent hold onto his office, or a challenger unseat him. You can find high political office-holders or challengers at campaign headquarters, but you can probably talk to candidates for the state legislature and lower offices at their homes.

Accept as large a responsibility as you can. If your candidate wins, your party will take note of you as a player in the successful election. In time you may become a party officer, delegate to a national convention, or even a candidate yourself. The party will owe you something, when you have faithfully supported its cause and candidates. One more thing. Want to know the best way onto a congressional staff in Washington? Have the foresight to back a challenger about to unseat an incumbent, and play a major role in the winning campaign.

INFORMATION

For general news awareness, the early pages of Chapter 7 offer suggestions. What evangelicals really need, however, is a source of information that deals with their particular interests. A source that focuses on the evangelical agenda found in the latter pages of Chapter 7, and matters not typically appearing on the front pages of the *New York Times* or the *Washington Post*.

Such a source will be timely, reliable, and trustworthy, and never written from a perspective of paranoia. It will have precise titles for legislation and specific House and Senate bill numbers. It will cover the full range of issues important to churches and their people, not simply the higher profile, inflammatory issues with good fund-raising potential.

For more than sixteen years now, the monthly four-page *NAE Washington Insight* newsletter has met those criteria and inspired trust. It is available by subscription @ $15/year, or as one of a package of benefits to individual members of NAE @ $30/year. A shorter, bulletin insert-sized church edition of *Insight* is also available in quantities for distribution through church bulletins or mailings. For information, write NAE office for Governmental Affairs, 1023 15th Street NW, Suite 500, Washington, DC 20005. Telephone 202/789-1011.

WASHINGTON ADDRESSES

The President
The White House
Washington, DC 20500
Dear Mr. President:

The Honorable (Name)
United States Senate
Washington, DC 20510
Dear Senator (Name)

The Honorable (Name)
House of Representatives
Washington, DC 20515
Dear Mr., Mrs. or Ms. (Name)

Note that House and Senate office building names and room numbers are not necessary. Each house of Congress has its own post office as does the White House.

SOMETHING TO THINK ABOUT

I am indebted to colleague Tim Crater for suggesting that evangelicals ponder the day when God determined to anoint a young shepherd to be king of Israel. Can anyone, in his wildest imagination, picture David responding, "No thank you, Lord—I'm not interested in politics"?

About twenty-eight centuries later, the Lord of history guided America's founders, in answer to prayer, to devise a nation in which the people would freely choose their leaders. In a marvelous twist, the rulers would be servants of the people, not the reverse. Since God Almighty providentially made it possible for us to rule ourselves, it would be equally unthinkable for evangelicals to say, "No thank you, Lord—I'm not interested in politics."

It would be unthinkable—wouldn't it?

POLITICAL ACTIVITY BY CLERGYMEN

ൟ

ALAN P. DYE, ESQ.,
WASHINGTON, D.C.

The IRS treatment of legislative and political activities by clergymen and organizations exempt from tax under Section 501(c)(3) of the Internal Revenue Code of 1986 (the Code) is subject to changing IRS interpretations, and it is dangerous to generalize based upon specific cases. Nevertheless, certain general principles may be relied upon with reasonable certainty. These are summarized below, along with the answers to some frequently asked questions. This article should not be interpreted as legal advice concerning any particular situation. Clergymen should consult their own tax advisors with respect to their particular circumstances.

LAW AND REGULATIONS

An organization is exempt from tax under Section 501(c)(3) if it is:

> …a corporation…fund, or foundation, organized and operated exclusively for religious,

> charitable, scientific, testing for public safety,
> literary, or educational purposes, . . . no part of
> the net earnings of which inures to the benefit
> of any private shareholder or individual, no
> substantial part of the activities of which is car-
> rying on propaganda, or otherwise attempting
> to influence legislation (except as provided in
> subsection [h]), and which does not participate
> in, or intervene in (including the publishing
> and distributing of statements), any political
> campaign on behalf of any candidate for public
> office.

It is apparent from the language of the statute that an *organization* exempt from tax under Section 501(c)(3) may undertake
no activity whatever on behalf of or in opposition to any candidate for public office—federal, state, or local. This is an absolute
prohibition.

Legislative activities, as contrasted to political activities, are
permissible for such an organization. However, the statute specifically prescribes that no *substantial part* of the activities of such
an organization may be devoted to activities intended to influence legislation.

The IRS regulations under Section 501(c)(3) elaborate on
the general statutory requirements as follows:

> *Authorization of legislative or political activities.*
> An organization is not organized exclusively for
> one or more exempt purposes if its articles
> expressly empower it:

(i) To devote more than an insubstantial part of its activities to attempting to influence legislation by propaganda or otherwise; or

(ii) Directly or indirectly to participate in, or intervene in (including the publishing or distributing of statements), any political campaign on behalf of or in opposition to any candidate for public office; or

(iii) To have objectives and to engage in activities which characterize it as an "action" organization as defined in paragraph (c)(3) of this section.

Sections 1.501(c)(3)-1(b)(3)(i) and (ii) of the above regulation merely restate Section 501(c)(3) and its prohibition of political activity and limitations on legislative activity, but subsection (iii) expands the limitations placed upon charitable or educational organizations to preclude Section 501(c)(3) status for so-called "action" organizations, which are defined to include any organization which contacts or urges the public to contact legislators regarding legislation or which itself advocates the adoption or rejection of legislation.

The statute does not define the term "substantial" for purposes of determining whether an organization qualifies under Section 501(c)(3). Court cases have held that an organization may devote at least 5 percent of its activities to lobbying without losing its tax-favored status, and that an organization devoting more than 20 percent of its activities to lobbying does not qualify.

Organizations devoting between 5 and 20 percent of their activities to such pursuits are in an area of uncertainty. The IRS has never accepted the applicability of any specific percentage to determine the substantiality of any organization's legislative activity.

In 1976, Code Section 501(h) was enacted to relieve some of this uncertainty. That section sets forth a procedure whereby an organization may elect to expend a specified portion of its budget for legislative activities without any adverse effect upon its tax-exempt status. The amount of such activity is computed on a statutorily prescribed sliding scale. As an example, an organization whose total expenditures on all exempt purposes are less than $500,000 per year may devote up to 20 percent of such expenditures to lobbying without paying any tax, and up to 30 percent without losing its tax-exempt status. Expenditures exceeding 20 percent, but less than 30 percent, are subject to a special tax, but will not adversely affect tax-exempt status.

Under Section 501(h), one-quarter of the allowable expenditure amount may be devoted to so-called "grassroots lobbying," defined as attempts to influence the general public regarding legislation. Organizations not electing under Section 501(h) are subject to the old rules. In either case, permissible lobbying must be in the public interest.

Section 501(h) may be elected by most organizations qualifying for tax exemption under Section 501(c)(3) of the Internal Revenue Code. However, while the bill was being considered by Congress, there were those in the church community who believed that churches are not subject to the prohibitions against lobbying in any respect. These organizations believed that to include churches and integrated auxiliaries of churches in the relief legislation would imply that the government had the right to revoke their tax exemptions if they engaged in legislative activity. Since they do not believe that this is true, the organizations lobbied for a provision excluding them from the benefits of 501(h). The result is that churches, integrated auxiliaries of churches, and members of affiliated groups in which one or more members are churches or integrated auxiliaries of churches are not eligible to elect the provision of Section 501(h). Religious institutions which are not churches or integrated auxiliaries can make this election.

The requirements of the statute may thus be summarized as follows: An organization carrying on public affairs activities may qualify for exemption from tax under Section 501(c)(3) and receive charitable contributions under Section 170(a) if its activities are educational, charitable, or religious; if it does not exceed the limitations imposed on lobbying and propaganda expenditures imposed by Section 501(c)(3) and/or Section 501(h); and if it engages in no activity intended to influence the election or defeat of any political candidate.

Federal elections are governed by Title 2 of the U.S. Code Section 431, *et seq.*, comprising the Federal Election Campaign Act of 1971, as amended. The election laws prohibit contributions or expenditures in connection with any federal campaign by any corporation. Since many churches and charities are incorporated, the prohibition extends to many such organizations. It should be noted that this prohibition extends only to "contributions" and "expenditures." Thus, directly or indirectly, a corporation must *spend money* in support of or opposition to a candidate before a violation can be found. Activity by a minister outside working hours would not constitute a contribution by his church, though political advocacy on church time might. Use of church facilities for a political purpose by a candidate or

264   Stand and Be Counted

committee may be the equivalent of a contribution, but merely allowing a visiting politician to deliver a sermon or read Scripture would not.

DISCUSSION

1. Endorsements

a. *Can a clergyman or office of a nonprofit tax-exempt organization publicly endorse a candidate for public office?*
    Neither the federal tax statutes nor the federal election law place impediments upon individuals expressing their election choices. The fact that a clergyman is employed by a tax-exempt organization does not destroy his personal constitutional right to political expression, and such an individual may personally endorse or oppose candidates for office without endangering the tax-exempt status of the organization by which he is employed.

b. *Can it be done from the premises or pulpit of the tax exempt organization?*
    There is no instance of which we are aware in which the Internal Revenue Service or the Federal Election Commission has sought to take adverse action against a church solely because its minister endorsed a candidate from the pulpit. However, a clergyman should not make a regular practice of endorsing candidates from the pulpit, lest his personal position be attributed to his church, and if he does choose to do so, he should make it clear to his congregation that the endorsement is a personal one and not that of the institution.

c. *Can the church or "organization" endorse a candidate?*
    No. Section 501(c)(3) of the Internal Revenue Code prohibits any direct or indirect participation in political campaigns

by a charitable or religious organization. This prohibition is broader than that of the election law, and extends to more than the mere expenditure of funds. Therefore, a charitable *organization* (including a church) which endorses a candidate for public office would be participating in a political campaign and would endanger its tax-exempt status.

d. *Can the clergyman or nonprofit organization leader/ officer lend his name to political advertisements and have his title listed under his name for identification purposes?*   Just as there is no prohibition against an individual employed by a tax-exempt organization engaging in political activity, there is no prohibition against the candidate using the individual's identification with such an organization if it is helpful in his candidacy. Clergymen who work on their own time in political campaigns may be identified by their organizational titles.

2. Voter Registration and Education

a. *Can a Section 501(c)(3) organization encourage or conduct voter registration or voter education activities among church members or on the nonprofit premises?*

Yes. The IRS has ruled that even private foundations may support voter education drives. See T.D. Release K-87, May 11, 1969. In this respect, IRS Revenue Ruling 78-248, states as follows:

> Certain "voter education" activities conducted in the nonpartisan manner may not constitute prohibited political activity under section 501(c)(3) of the Code. Other so-called "voter education" activities, however may be proscribed by the statute."

This revenue ruling contains a number of examples of situations illustrative of the rules as applied by the IRS. In one example, an organization compiled and made generally available to the public voting records of all members of Congress. The publication contained no editorial opinion, and its contents did not imply approval or disapproval of the members' voting records. The IRS held that such activity is not prohibited to a Section 501(c)(3) organization.

In another situation an organization was found to qualify as a Section 501(c)(3) organization even though it published a voters' guide containing the opinions of various candidates for political office on a wide variety of issues. It is important to note that the issues were selected solely on the basis of their importance and interest to the electorate as a whole. Candidates' positions were ascertained through answers to a questionnaire sent to all candidates.

Important distinctions may be drawn from a third example in which the same sort of questionnaire was sent to candidates in order to prepare a voters' guide, but the questionnaire was structured in such a way that it evidenced bias on certain issues. The organization was held not to qualify for tax-exempt status.

b. *Must voter registration activities be nonpartisan?*
Yes.

c. *Can the organization spend money for paying registration organizers or for mailing out registration forms?*
Yes, if the registration is nonpartisan.

3. Candidate Appearances

a. *Can candidates speak on the premises of a Section 501(c)(3) organization?*

The Internal Revenue Service has never to our knowledge attempted to revoke the tax-exempt status of an organization which has allowed political candidates to speak on the premises. It is fairly clear that there is no problem with such practice if all candidates are allowed to speak, rather than merely those endorsed by the leaders of the institution. This is consistent with revenue rulings dealing with broadcasting stations, in which it has been held that providing reasonable air time to all legally qualified candidates for election to public office does not constitute participation in a political campaign. See Rev. Rel. 74-574, 1974-2 C.B. 160.

The question is a closer one if only certain candidates are allowed to address the group with political speeches. It could, of course, be argued that allowing a candidate to speak involves no expenditure or endorsement by the organization or that purely internal communications do not constitute intervention in a political campaign. Further, as we have noted, we know of no instance in which an organization has lost its tax-exempt status for such activities. Nevertheless, more care and consideration should be given to such an activity than to an activity where all candidates are provided with the opportunity to speak.

Of course, candidates and public officials retain their rights to religious expression. Ministers should be safe in introducing a candidate present in the congregation at a service, and candidates who are members of a congregation may be allowed to deliver sermons and read Scripture.

b. *Can a public incumbent office-holder speak on the premises or from the pulpit?*

Yes, though if such office holders are candidates, the same considerations apply as are discussed above.

c. *Can an organization exempt from tax under Section 501(c)(3) operate forums where all candidates for a particular office come and speak?*

Though the Internal Revenue Service has apparently never ruled on this exact question, such an activity is consistent with other IRS rulings. See, for instance, Revenue Ruling 74-574, *supra*, involving appearances by candidates on television stations operated by religious and educational groups. See, also, Revenue Ruling 66-256, 1966-2 C.B. 210, in which an organization was held to qualify for Section 501(c)(3) status where it conducted public forums at which elections and debates on social, political, and international matters are presented.

4. Fund Raising

Can funds be raised at religious services for campaign contributions to candidates, contributions to political parties, or contributions for a legislative battle or moral or educational issue campaign?

An organization may qualify for Section 501(c)(3) status so long as it does not devote a *substantial* portion of its activities to propaganda or legislative activities. Collecting money at a church service does not involve an expenditure of funds which could under any circumstances amount to a substantial expenditure. Therefore, allowing fund-raising for lobbying campaigns at church services incurs no significant expense.

In contrast, raising money for a candidate or political party would constitute indirect participation in a political campaign. Since the prohibition on such activities is absolute, such an activity could result in the loss of tax-exempt status.

5. Mailing Lists

Can an organization exempt from tax under Section 501(c)(3) loan or rent its mailing list to an organization carrying on legislative activities or to a candidate or political committee for campaign fund-raising?

Both the Federal Election Commission and the Internal Revenue Service would react adversely to a loan of an organization's mailing list for use in a political campaign. Such an activity would constitute a corporate political expenditure to the extent that corporate funds had been used to develop the membership list. It would also constitute participation in a political campaign for purposes of Section 501(c)(3).

The loan of a mailing list to a "legislative" organization must be analyzed using different principles. The election law would not apply since that statute applies only to political activities rather than legislative ones. The loan could be considered a legislative expenditure to the extent of the cost of providing it, but in any event would be considered such an expenditure only to the extent of any additional cost incurred by the corporation. Presumably, such additional costs would be very slight and would only in a very unusual circumstance result in substantial expenditure.

It is clear that both political candidates and parties and legislative organizations can buy mailing lists from charitable organizations. No problem would exist in any of the above cases if the list were rented at its fair market value (the value at which it is rented to other organizations, if at all) to either a political organization or a legislative organization.

We have attempted to deal in general summary form with problems that commonly arise. The reader should recognize, however, that the tax effect of political or legislative activity on a church or charity depends on the precise facts of the particular case. Each church should consult its own counsel with respect to its specific activities.

Revised September 1994

Notes

1. Charles W. Colson, *Kingdoms in Conflict* (Grand Rapids: Mich.: Morrow/Zondervan, 1987), 306f.

2. Dr. Howard mailed me a copy of his address as published in *Vital Speeches.*

3. Alistair Cooke, *America* (New York: Alfred A. Knopf, 1974), 136.

4. Quoted in Steve Halliday and Al Janssen, eds., *Carl Henry at His Best* (Portland, Oregon: Multnomah Press), 46.

5. Charles W. Colson, *Against the Night: Living in the New Dark Ages* (Ann Arbor, Mich.: Servant Publications, 1989), 9-11.

6. George W. Cornell, "Theologian Fears for the Future of Democracy," *Washington Post,* 24 October, 1992.

7. William J.Bennett, "Revolt Against God: America's Spiritual Despair," *Policy Review,* Winter 1994, 23.

8. Copies of this report, updated annually, may be ordered from The Heritage Foundation, 214 Massachusetts Avenue, NE, Washington, DC 20002-4999.

9. Os Guinness, *The American Hour: A Time of Reckoning and the Once and Future Role of Faith* (New York: The Free Press, 1993), 111.

10. Thomas C. Oden, *After Modernity, What?* (Grand Rapids, Mich.: Zondervan Publishing House, 1992), 36.

11. *Wall Street Journal,* 15 June, 1993.

12. Family Research Council publication, *Insight,* June, 1993.

13. "Telling it straight," *Washington Times,* 20 April 1993.

14. Statement made during address of Biennial NAE Washington Insight Briefing, April 1994.

CHAPTER TWO

1. Cardinal John O'Connor and Mayor Ed Koch, *His Eminence and Hizzoner* (New York: Morrow, 1989).

2. McDaniel v. Paty, U. S. Supreme Court Reports, 1977, 435 US 618.

3. In one court case, an organization devoting 5 percent of its activities to lobbying did not lose its tax-exempt status, while in another case, an organization devoting more than 20 percent of its activities to lobbying was disqualified from 501(c)(3) status.

4. Sadly, gay rights activists persisted, pouring large amounts of money into the fray, and reversed that result in 1990. For the most part, homosexuals have higher than average incomes and no family for whom they are financially responsible. Acceptance of their lifestyle is their all-consuming interest.

CHAPTER THREE

1. *Political Debates Between Honorable Abraham Lincoln and Honorable Stephen A. Douglas* (Columbus, Ohio: Follet, Foster & Co., 1800), 82.

2. Since 1992, the Office for Governmental Affairs of the National Association of Evangelicals has offered materials to help churches do just that. Its *Manual for Action,* updated every two years, can help launch a Christian Citizenship Ministry in your church.

CHAPTER FOUR

1. For my understanding of the theology of the kingdom of God, I am primarily indebted to the late New Testament scholar George Eldon Ladd. It was my privilege to take several of his courses in Biblical Theology at Fuller Theological Seminary from 1953-57.

2. George E. Ladd, *Crucial Questions About the Kingdom of God* (Grand Rapids, Mich.: Wm. B. Eerdmans, 1952), 25.

3. Ibid., 80.

4. I devote Chapter 9 to the intent of America's Founding Fathers to establish the United States as "one nation under God."

CHAPTER FIVE

1. "Why Celebrate the Constitution?" Mark W. Cannon, *The Constitution*, September 1985, 22.

2. Ibid., 20.

3. Robert L. Cord, *Separation of Church and State: Historical Fact and Current Fiction* (New York: Lambeth Press, 1982), 86. Following letter on same page.

4. Ibid., 4.

5. See my article on "Preserving the Role of the State," Platform Plank #2, *Eternity*, October 1987, 25.

6. For detail on the pivotal *Everson v. Board of Education* decision refer to Chapter 11.

7. Cord, 198f.

8. *Congressional Quarterly Weekly Report*, 8 June, 1985, 1114.

9. Information about the Charter is available through The First Liberty Institute, Department of Curriculum and Instruction, George Mason University, 4400 University Drive, Fairfax, VA 22030.

10. Pages 12, 16, and 19.

11. "Keeping God in the Closet—Some Thoughts on the Exorcism of Religious Values from Public Life," Representative Henry J. Hyde. Speech given September 24, 1984 at Notre Dame Law School.

12. Acts 22:25-29, most of chapters 25 and 26, and 28:17-20.

CHAPTER SIX

1. The four-page *NAE Washington Insight* newsletter is sent to NAE member churches, individuals, or organizations. It is also available by subscription. A special church edition of "Insight" can be ordered in bulk quantities for distribution in churches and elsewhere. Write for information to the National Association of Evangelicals, Box 28, Wheaton, Illinois 60189. Or, should you prefer, write to NAE Office for Governmental Affairs, 1023 15th Street, Suite 500, Washington, DC 20005.

2. So troubled was the Evangelical Free Church by the stance of its most prominent layman that it editorialized officially that Anderson was at odds with his own church.

3. Richard A. Viguerie, *The New Right: We're Ready to Lead* (Falls Church, Va.: The Viguerie Company, 1981), 123f.

4. Ibid., 128.

5. Many of those same evangelicals regard Jimmy Carter as the finest ex-president in their lifetime. They had always respected his personal piety, his verbal witness, and his commitment to the church as manifested in serving as a regular Sunday school teacher even while president. Today there is even more to admire: his refusal to exploit the presidency for personal gain, his servant-role in working with Habitat for Humanity, and his persistent efforts for peace.

6. Text of Mrs. Reagan's remarks as released by the White House press office, July 27, 1988.

CHAPTER SEVEN

1. Richard Cizik, ed. *The High Cost of Indifference* (Ventura, Cal.: Regal Books, 1984).

2. The National Association of Evangelicals has for more than seventeen years published a four-page monthly newsletter, *NAE*

Washington Insight. It has a reputation for being objective, timely, and accurate, and is not written from a perspective of paranoia. A shorter, bulletin insert-sized church edition of *Insight* is also available for bulk distribution in church services or mailings. Write NAE Office for Governmental Affairs, 1023 15th street NW, Suite 500, Washington, DC 20005 for sample copies and subscription information.

3. To write the President: The President, The White House, Washington, DC 20500, Dear Mr. President. To write a Senator: The Honorable (Name), United States Senate, Washington, DC 20510, Dear Senator (Name). To write a Congressperson: The Honorable (Name), House of Representatives, Washington, DC 20515, Dear (Mr., Ms., or Mrs.) (Name). The best close is Sincerely yours. Note that street addresses, building names, and room numbers are unnecessary. Congress has its own post office and it delivers speedily.

4. Cizik, *The High Cost of Indifference,* 195.

5. John W. Montgomery, "The Limits of Christian Influence," Current Religious Thought column in *Christianity Today,* 23 January, 1981.

6. Forest D. Montgomery, "One Nation Under God" (Wheaton, Ill.: NAE, 1986).

7. Benjamin Weiss, *God in American History* (Grand Rapids, Mich.: Zondervan, 1966), 92.

8. "The Virginia Citizen," January 1994, V-3.

9. Charles W. Colson, "Putting Justice Together Again," *Justice Report* (Winter 1990).

10. Robert Rector, quoted in "The Not-So-Great Society," Larry Burkett, *World,* 21 May 1994.

11. Robert Holland, "Racial Rigged Job Test Scores," *Washington Times,* 7 June 1990, F1.

12. Editorial in *USA Today*, 17 June 1994, 18A and *U.S. News & World Report*, 1 August 1994, 6.

13. Justice Fellowship, an affiliate of Charles Colson's Prison Fellowship, seeks "to restore balance to the criminal justice system by focusing on reforms which address the needs of victims." While JF believes that society must be protected from violent offenders, it argues that non-dangerous offenders should be sentenced to restitution and community service programs rather than prison." For ten years I served on the Board of Directors of Justice Fellowship, P.O. Box 17181, Washington, DC 20041-0181.

14. "Illegitimacy: An unprecedented Catastrophe," *Washington Post*, 22 June 1994.

15. "A Mom and Pop Manifesto," Henry Hyde, *Policy Review*, Spring 1994, 29.

16. William Raspberry, "Family Stories," *Washington Post*, 29 July 1990.

17. Jack Kemp, "A Cultural Renaissance," *Imprimis*, a publication of Hillsdale College, August 1994.

CHAPTER EIGHT

1. Franklin D. Roosevelt deserves an asterisk for his 523 votes in 1936. There were only 48 states in those days, and he carried all but the 8 electoral votes from Maine and Vermont combined.

2. "With Polish, Maybe—J. Winston Quayle?" *World*, 26 September 1989, 9.

3. Technically, the Democrats had 58 seats and Virginia's Harry Byrd was an Independent. Byrd always voted with the Democrats to organize the Senate, however, so I include him in their number here.

4. Robert A. Caro, *The Years of Lyndon Johnson: Means of Ascent* (New York: Alfred A. Knopf, 1990).

CHAPTER NINE

1. Education Update, Heritage Foundation, vol. 10, no. 3, Summer 1987.

2. Robert L. Cord, *Separation of Church and State: Historical Fact and Current Fiction* (New York: Lambeth Press, 1982), 5lf.

3. Benjamin Weiss, *God In American History* (Grand Rapids, Mich., Zondervan, 1966), 51f.

4. John Eidsmoe, *Christianity and the Constitution* (Grand Rapids, Mich.: Baker Book House, 1987).

5. James A. Reichley, *Religion in American Public Life* (Washington, D.C., Brookings Institution, 1985) p. 104.

6. Ibid., 105.

7. Congressional Record, July 18, 1990, S 9885.

8. Reichley, p. 94.

9. Ibid., 88.

10. John Tyler, Millard Fillmore, Andrew Johnson, and Chester Arthur.

11. Bob Arnebeck, "FDR Invoked God, Too," *Washington Post,* 21 September 1986.

12. I am well aware of the scholarly debate, even among evangelicals, over the nature of America's spiritual heritage. In their book, *The Search for Christian America,* authors Mark Noll, Nathan Hatch, and George Marsden argue that early America does not deserve to be called Christian, and that such an idea is at best an ambiguous concept. On the other hand, in his *Defending the Declaration,* Gary Amos is "horrified" at the conclusions of Noll, Hatch, and Marsden's book.

278   Stand and Be Counted

13. President Washington made a similar treaty with the Oneida, Tuscarora and Stockbridge Indians in January 1795.

14. Barnes frequently appears on network public affairs television shows. He had a privileged hour in the sun during the first Reagan-Mondale television debate of the 1984 campaign. As a member of the panel of questioners, he asked whether either candidate was a born-again Christian. Fred had recently come to Christian faith at that time and was not trying to throw the candidates a curve but to elicit a positive confession of faith if that were possible. Both Reagan and Mondale managed to dodge the question.

15. *PS*, a publication of the American Political Science Association, Fall 1986, 801-806.

CHAPTER TEN

1. Henry J. Hyde, "The Culture War" *National Review*, 30 April 1990, 25.

2. *Time*, Interview with David Aikman, 24 July 1989, 60.

3. *Cultural Conservatism—Toward a New National Agenda* (Washington, DC: Free Congress Research and Education Foundation), 4.

4. Eidsmoe, *Christianity and the Constitution*, 295.

5. Memorandum dated April 18, 1990, Free Congress Foundation.

6. *Time*, Interview with David Aikman, 24 July 1989, 60.

7. Bruce L. Shelley, *The Gospel and the American Dream* (Portland, Ore.: Multnomah Press, 1989), 109.

8. Josh McDowell, "The Gap Widens," *Eternity*, June 1987, 15.

9. Charles W. Colson's speech to the National Religious Broadcasters, January 29, 1994, 3.

10. John Leo, "Boxing in Believers," *U.S. News & World Report,* 20 September 1993, 20. He writes re: Stephen Carter's book *The Culture of Disbelief.*

11. Terri Graves Taylor, *Genesis* newsletter, 9 April 1990, 6f.

12. See "Feminism and the College Curriculum," Christina Hoff Sommers, *Imprimis,* June 1990.

13. *NAE Washington Insight* newsletter, January 1984.

14. Katherine Kirsten, "How the Feminist Establishment Hurts Women," 20 June1994, 20.

15. Speech given by Weigel, president of Washington's Ethics and Public Policy Center, at NAE Washington Insight Briefing, 1990.

16. Paul Weyrich, *Cultural Conservatism, Toward a New National Agenda* (Washington, D.C., Free Congress Research and Education Foundation, 1988).

17. Randy Alcorn, *Eternal Perspectives* newsletter, April-May 1994, 5.

18. Media bias on the abortion issue was undeniably demonstrated by a July 1-4, 1990 series of articles in the *Los Angeles Times.* We noticed a significant admission along those lines weeks before, when the *Washington Post's* ombudsman admitted that his paper had not distinguished itself with its biased reporting on pro-life events.

19. Kenneth A. Myers, "Holy Excrement," *Genesis,* 9 April 1990.

20. Reported in the *Washington Post,* 13 October 1987.

21. The line of reasoning in this paragraph is found in Donald L. Faris, "Gay Attempts at Revising Our Language, *Theology & Ethics,* in *The Standard,* 3 Quarter 1994, published by Exodus International.

22. Cal Thomas, "Sex and Lies," On Videotape, World 15 January 1994.

23. Rolf Zettersten, "Something Worth Saving Again," in *Focus on the Family* magazine, September 1989, 23.

24. Joseph Sobran, quoted in *Summit Journal*, March 1992, 4.

25. *Living with Our Differences: Religious Liberty in a Pluralistic Society*, First Liberty Institute (Boston, Mass.: Learning Connections Publishers, Inc., 1990), upper elementary edition 183.

26. Charles W. Colson, "America Is Not a Christian Nation," counter-point article in *Light*, November-December 1993.

27. *National & International Religion Report*, 2 May 1994, 7.

28. "The Tuned Out Generation," *Time*, July 1990, 80.

29. Interview in *Charisma & Christian Life*, July 1990, 80.

30. Wead's response in that regard was followed by this sentence, however. "Now that is not true of all evangelical lobbies. There are three powerful ones in town. The National Association of Evangelicals has been around the longest time and covers a very wide range of issues." Doug went on to include Concerned Women for America and the Family Research Council in his honor roll.

31. *Carl Henry at His Best*, (Portland, Ore.: Multnomah Press), 46.